How the World Wide Web Works

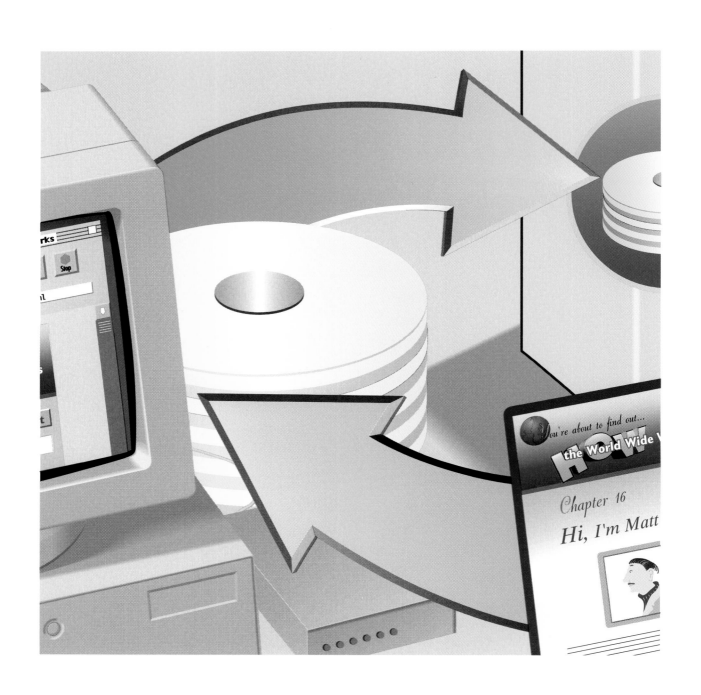

How the World Wide Web Works

Chris Shipley and Matt Fish

Illustrated by Mina Reimer

Ziff-Davis Press
An imprint of Macmillan Computer Publishing USA
Emeryville, California

Acquisitions Editor	Suzanne Anthony
Development Editor	Valerie Haynes Perry
Copy Editor	Margo Hill
Technical Reviewer	Tom Baker
Project Coordinator	Ami Knox
Cover Illustration and Design	Megan Gandt
Book Design	Carrie English and Bruce Lundquist
Illustrators	Mina Reimer and Sarah Ishida
Word Processing	Howard Blechman
Page Layout	Bruce Lundquist
Indexer	Julie Kawabata

Ziff-Davis Press, ZD Press, and the Ziff-Davis Press logo are trademarks or registered trademarks of, and are licensed to Macmillan Computer Publishing USA by Ziff-Davis Publishing Company, New York, New York.

Ziff-Davis Press imprint books are produced on a Macintosh computer system with the following applications: FrameMaker®, Microsoft® Word, QuarkXPress®, Adobe Illustrator®, Adobe Photoshop®, Adobe Streamline™, MacLink®*Plus*, Aldus® FreeHand™, Collage Plus™.

Ziff-Davis Press, an imprint of
Macmillan Computer Publishing USA
5903 Christie Avenue
Emeryville, CA 94608

ISBN 1-56276-369-5

Manufactured in the United States of America

10 9 8 7 6 5 4 3 2 1

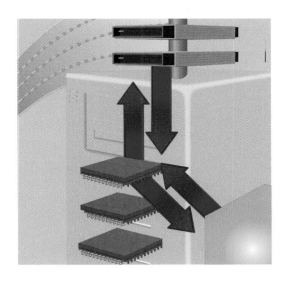

For our (respective) parents.

Two people wrote this book, but it could never have been finished without the enduring patience of many people. The first order of thanks goes to Suzanne Anthony for roping me into this project, then kindly not using the spare length of line to strangle me when the inevitable delays ensued. Thanks also to Matt for climbing aboard the speeding train and riding it into the station with me, and to Tom Baker who provided many a lively debate and caught more than a few oversights in his review of the drafts. Again, it has been my pleasure to work with Valerie Haynes Perry and Ami Knox, who with true professionalism shepherded this book through its development and production; it's much better for having them on the team. Finally, I must acknowledge the generous encouragements of friends, especially Nancy, Julie, and Kim, who with great compassion asked time and again, "Aren't you done with that %@!&* book yet?" and drove me on to the finish line.

—*Chris Shipley*

What she said. Plus, she forgot to mention all those people who are working and writing on the Web and sharing what they've learned with people like us so that we can share it with you.

I also would like to thank Chris for the opportunity and camaraderie, Brian Howell and Brian Topping for sharing their brains with me (scary), and Tom Baker for helping me look smart. Thanks to Good-Time Charleena for providing the incentive to finish, the whole gang at 26 Hugo Street, everybody at Trout Lake in June, Toby Lathrop for nothing, Jean Wood and her furry friends, Erik and Erika, Mert Fish (1940–1995), Ginger, Kori and Becky, and the rest of my family. Special thanks to John Wood for inspiring me to take risks and for getting me started on this journey in the first place.

—*Matt Fish*

FOR some reason known only to book publishers, the introduction to a book is the *last* thing to be written. It so happened that the deadline for this bit of text coincided exactly with Spring Internet World 1996. Two years ago, this conference and exhibition barely filled half the exhibit space of the San Jose Convention Center. Exhibitors in pre-fab booths pushed e-mail software and talked about newsgroups and FTP sites. There was only a little bit of chat about an emerging technology called the World Wide Web. Today, Internet World spills onto the streets of San Jose. Display tents have been pitched on neighboring lots. Hotels are overflowing with press conferences and even nearby galleries are hosting exhibits and meetings. And for all intents and purposes, it looks like the show ought to be called "Web World."

The explosive growth of interest in the World Wide Web is evident these days in San Jose and around the globe. With unprecedented speed, the Web has become a vital and pervasive technology for information sharing, research, communication, and commerce. And if the enthusiasm, optimism, and just plain smarts that shined through at Internet World are any indication, the growth is just beginning.

Whether you are an individual interested in learning more about the Web as a tool for gathering information, or someone seeking to use the Web to deliver information, this book is designed for you. In the next 24 chapters, you'll learn the fundamentals of Web technology and gain new insights and ideas about how to use the Web for personal or professional pursuits.

The Web wave is by no means cresting, so dive into this book, learn how the World Wide Web works, and begin surfing like a pro.

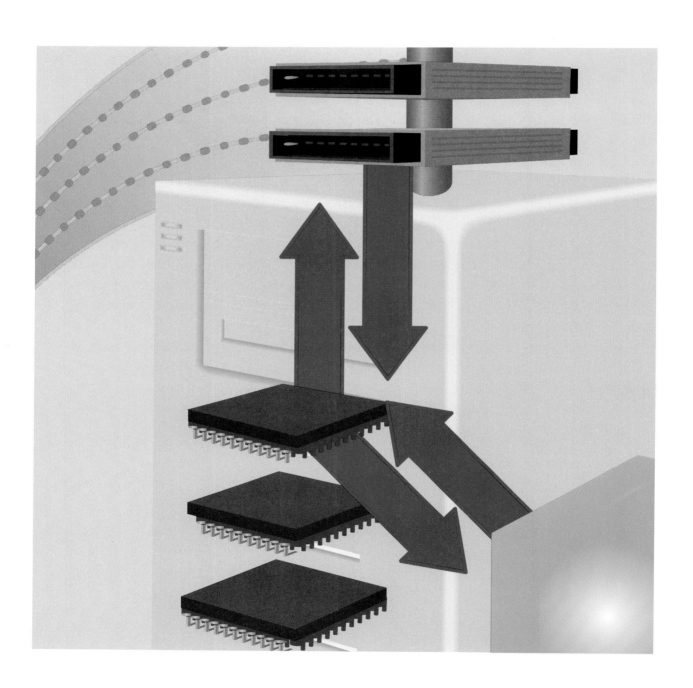

P A R T

BUILDING BLOCKS OF THE WORLD WIDE WEB

UNLESS

you've been far away from any developed country for the last year or so, you've heard about the World Wide Web. But just what is this Web? Technically, it's a huge distributed hypertext document. But what does *that* mean?

Imagine, if you will, a giant book consisting of millions and millions of pages. Now imagine the binding has come loose from that book and chunks of pages have been stored in libraries throughout the world. Now imagine if, from any one of those libraries, you could reach out to another library and grab another sheaf of pages. Stretch your mind just a little bit more and imagine that anywhere in the world, individuals and groups can create and add more pages to that book, store them in their local libraries, and connect those libraries into the network of libraries that house the other pages.

If you can envision this scenario, you are beginning to have a pretty good idea of just how the World Wide Web works. But it would be inaccurate to think that the book is a neatly written, text-filled tome exhaustively covering a single, albeit broad, subject. The Web is better thought of as a vast collection of books—thousands and thousands of them—covering every imaginable subject. And these "books" aren't written by professional journalists, noted authors, or respected publishing houses (at least not many of them are); they're written by researchers, students, scientists, marketing executives, government officials, and thousands of computer-enthused, Internet-enabled individuals.

The World Wide Web is a system of documents that can be retrieved and viewed by anyone anywhere in the world who has access to the Internet. (The same technology can also be used to distribute documents within an organization, a concept called the Intranet.) This system links any document to any other document stored anywhere else on the system. In late 1994, about 20,000 host computers had registered domain names in order to be a part of this document exchange system. Today, that number is well over 100,000, and it's doubling about once every two months. And these domains host tens of millions of documents worldwide.

This explosive growth comes, in part, because the World Wide Web represents a new publishing medium that is easily accessed by large and small companies, private businesses, government agencies, academia, and—perhaps most important—private individuals. Many people think of the Web as a place much like a library. It is that, certainly, but it is also more than that. It is a new medium, a machine for presenting ideas, images, and more: Sounds and movies and software can all be published and distributed on the Web. Thousands of organizations and individuals are delivering their messages to millions of readers through this new medium. Some people are presenting research results, sharing vital new data with colleagues around the globe. Others are publishing their poetry, novellas, and songs for audiences who might not otherwise have the opportunity to see these new works. Some people use the Web to advertise, sell, and support their products and services. And there are plenty of people who are presenting ideas and writings that are just plain weird. Today, anyone with an idea, a computer, a word processor, a modem, and Internet access or an online service membership can tap into the vanity press that is the World Wide Web.

At first blush, the Web seems like a complex intertwining of obscure protocols and technical magic. In fact, it's that perception that has discouraged many people from using the Internet and the Web. Certainly, the Web and the Internet it rides upon do rely on communications protocols that enable systems to talk with one another and exchange information. But to the typical Web explorer, and even to those who aspire to create and post their own sites, the Web—when broken down into its component parts—is really rather simple.

As you read this book, you'll discover how this Web works. You'll learn the lingo, see how documents are interwoven, and gain an understanding of the tools you'll need in order to explore the vast library of documents that reside on the Web. Along the way, you'll no doubt also have a few ideas about how you can publish on the Web yourself. Sure, if you want to create a complex Web-based service, you'll need more than a little programming know-how. And we'll address some of that know-how later in this book. For now, though, let's look at the basic anatomy of the Web.

The problem, of course, is that people tend to use lots of different terms to mean basically the same thing, and occasionally the same term to mean different things. Page. Document. Home page. Site. URL. Address. Domain. Server. Hypertext. HTML. Markup language. In the following pages, we will reveal the mysteries of these and other terms, and we will break the Web down piece by piece, explaining each one.

Remember, though, that while we'll discuss each piece separately, each of the Web's components is interdependent on the other. As each chapter illuminates the details of the Web, bear in mind that an aggregate understanding of how the Web works is dependent on knowing its parts in some detail. Rest assured that by the time you're through with this section, you'll have a clear understanding of how each piece works—and how they all work together.

CHAPTER

1

The Web and the Internet

IN the beginning—and in this story the beginning wasn't that long ago—there was the Internet, a computer network linking other computer networks in an intricate and—most importantly—reliable communications system. In the 30-odd years since it began, the story has become familiar to most anyone involved with computers.

The progeny of a U.S. Department of Defense project to link military and research computer systems in a fail-safe network, the Internet was designed during the Cold War to prevent a single nuclear strike from disabling all military computer capability. The Internet grew into a super-network interconnecting computers at universities, government and military offices, and research centers around the world. A system of advanced protocols tells these computers how to locate and exchange data with one another, passing information from computer to computer as the system seeking information reaches the system that houses the desired data. Packets of information are detoured around nonoperative systems, if necessary, until the information finds its way to the proper destination. So, for example, a simple e-mail message could travel from Chicago in several packets, each traveling a different electronic route, until they reach their destination on Long Island and they are reassembled into a single message.

The Internet proved to be a remarkable way for people to communicate and share information, but in its native form it was a system so ugly that only its creators could love it. Those who used the system needed a working knowledge of the UNIX operating system in order to tap into the network. This interface was so nonintuitive that only computer specialists could navigate the Internet, and thus many people who would have benefited from the data housed in the system were unable to access it.

There had to be a better way to find and retrieve documents, and in 1989 a couple of researchers at a physics particle-accelerator laboratory in Geneva, Switzerland, conceived of it. Tim Berners-Lee and his associates at the research center known as CERN (the French acronym for The European Laboratory for Particle Physics) invented a series of communications protocols that would present information in documents that could be linked to other documents and stored on computers throughout the Internet. People could access these documents, or "pages," through a single software program, called a browser. The system was called the World Wide Web, also known as WWW, W3, or simply—and as we'll use throughout this book—the Web.

In the year that followed, Berners-Lee spearheaded the development of a Web prototype. The early Web was based on the concept of "distributed computing," which allowed an application or document to reside in parts across many computers. The first Web documents were text-only and the browser used to retrieve and view these documents was a crude text reader. Still, the system enabled researchers to locate one document on the Web and from the first document access remote documents elsewhere on the Web. This was possible without requiring the user to enter complicated retrieval commands—or even know where the related document resided.

The system developed at CERN was made publicly available, but was used initially by the scientific community as a means of distributing research findings. It wasn't until the National Center for Superconducting Applications (NCSA) released an early UNIX version of the Mosaic Web browser in 1993 that the broader community of academics and online enthusiasts began to explore the possibilities of the Web. Mosaic was the brainchild of Marc Andreessen, then a student at the University of Illinois at Urbana-Champaign and now a principal at Netscape, the hugely successful Internet software company. Andreessen's idea was to create a graphical interface to the Web. Unlike earlier Web browsers, Mosaic used icons, pull-down menus, bit-mapped graphics, and colorful links to display hypertext documents. Later that same year, versions of Mosaic were created for the Macintosh and Windows operating systems.

This graphical Web browser proved to be the match that set the Web on fire. In the two years since these personal computer-based versions of Mosaic made the scene, the Web has exploded into an information revolution and a cultural phenomenon. Mosaic, of course, isn't the end of the story—not by a long shot. There is little doubt that the Web is the fastest growing sector of the technology market. Andreessen's new company, Netscape, was one of the top three public offerings in the financial markets last year, and the Netscape browser is now in use by more than 30 million people worldwide. Today, there are hundreds of thousands of unique Web sites throughout the world, housing countless numbers of individual Web pages. Evidence suggests the number of Web sites now doubles every month or so.

But how does this World Wide Web work? To be clear, the Web is not a system separate from the Internet. Instead, it is a system that rides on top of the Internet. The Internet itself is a series of interconnected networks, in essence a network of networks. The Web is really a system of protocols exchanged between a *client* (your computer) and a *server* (the host computer's application that delivers Web pages) in order that documents can be shared among computers on the network.

If you didn't follow that last paragraph exactly, don't worry. As we proceed through this book, you'll learn about the protocols and software and new technologies that are working together to make the Web the most innovative new medium since television. Perhaps the best place to start, though, is at the Internet itself. In simplest terms, the Internet is made up of *host* computers linked together by a dedicated broadband telecommunications connection, known as the *backbone*. The connection is *dedicated*, because it is always "open." That is, once the computer is connected to the backbone, the connection is always active, just as if you took a telephone off the hook, made a call, and never hung up on that call. The connection is *broadband* in that it can transmit large amounts of data simultaneously. Other computers tap into the backbone by connecting to host computers linked directly to the Internet background, typically using connections that are somewhat slower that the high-speed T3 leased lines of the backbone. In turn, these computers connect to other computers, which in turn link to other computers, and so on, until you have a complicated network of computers all joined together, either over dedicated phone lines, or, as is the case with individual users at home, via dial-up lines.

With so many computers linking to the Internet, they need a common language to "talk" to one another. That language is a series of protocols that describe the data that is sent across the network and explain what to do with it when it reaches its destination. The most fundamental of Internet protocols is called TCP/IP, or Transmission Control Protocol/Internet Protocol. We'll talk more about TCP/IP in later chapters, but in short, TCP/IP is an envelope in which data resides. The TCP protocol tells computers what's in the envelope and the IP protocol tells computers where to send the package.

On top of this system of computers and connections is the Web. You can think of the Web as an application, much like a database, and think of the Internet as the operating system. In fact, the Web is an elaborate *distributed* database of documents, graphics, and other multimedia elements. As you "surf" the Web, you use a browser to request data from the database and to display that data when the request is fulfilled by the server that processes the request and sends the desired data back to your computer.

These pieces—the Internet "operating system" and the Web "application"—are illustrated on the following pages.

How the Web Rides on the Internet

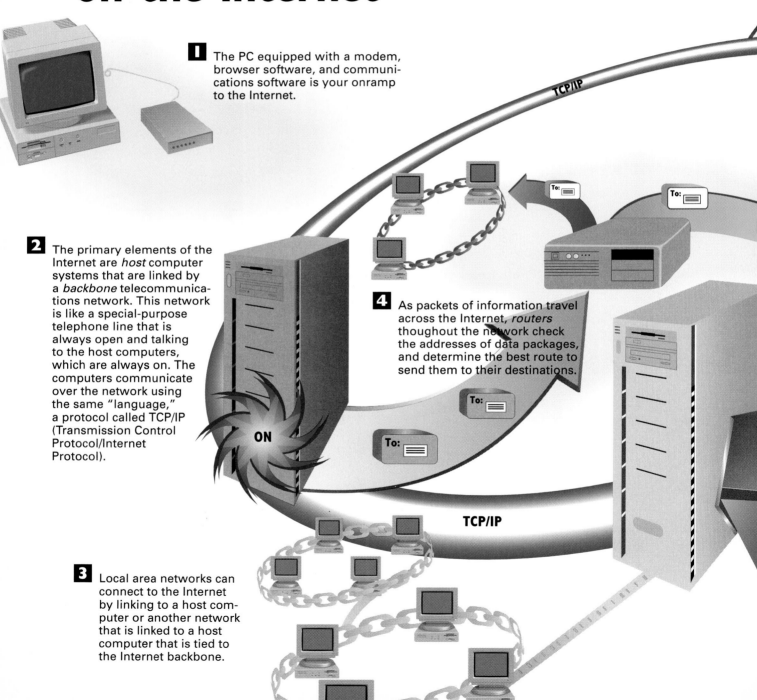

1 The PC equipped with a modem, browser software, and communications software is your onramp to the Internet.

2 The primary elements of the Internet are *host* computer systems that are linked by a *backbone* telecommunications network. This network is like a special-purpose telephone line that is always open and talking to the host computers, which are always on. The computers communicate over the network using the same "language," a protocol called TCP/IP (Transmission Control Protocol/Internet Protocol).

4 As packets of information travel across the Internet, *routers* thoughout the network check the addresses of data packages, and determine the best route to send them to their destinations.

3 Local area networks can connect to the Internet by linking to a host computer or another network that is linked to a host computer that is tied to the Internet backbone.

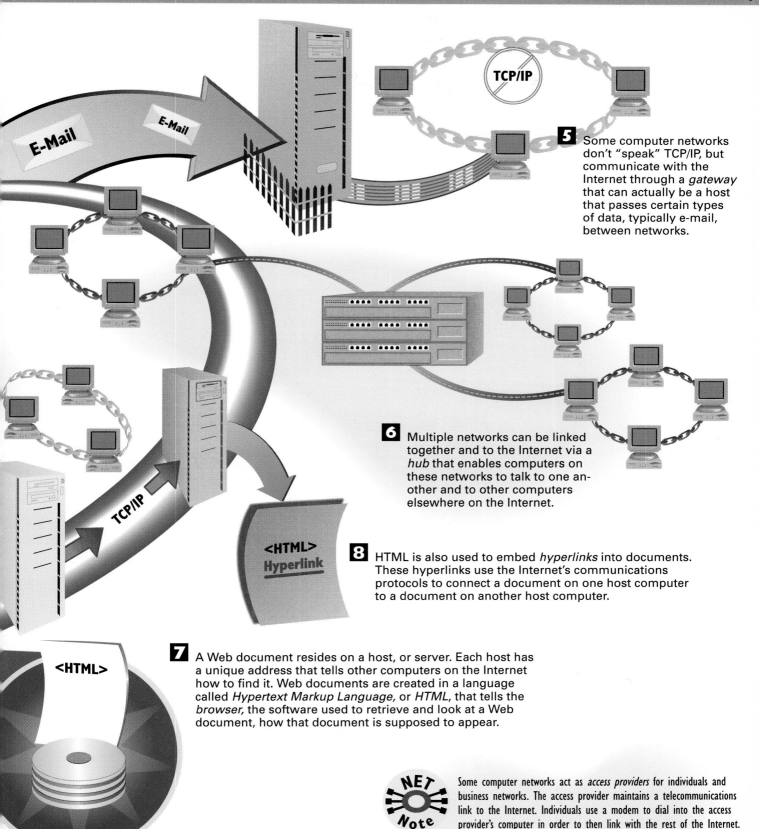

5 Some computer networks don't "speak" TCP/IP, but communicate with the Internet through a *gateway* that can actually be a host that passes certain types of data, typically e-mail, between networks.

6 Multiple networks can be linked together and to the Internet via a *hub* that enables computers on these networks to talk to one another and to other computers elsewhere on the Internet.

8 HTML is also used to embed *hyperlinks* into documents. These hyperlinks use the Internet's communications protocols to connect a document on one host computer to a document on another host computer.

7 A Web document resides on a host, or server. Each host has a unique address that tells other computers on the Internet how to find it. Web documents are created in a language called *Hypertext Markup Language,* or *HTML*, that tells the *browser*, the software used to retrieve and look at a Web document, how that document is supposed to appear.

NET Note Some computer networks act as *access providers* for individuals and business networks. The access provider maintains a telecommunications link to the Internet. Individuals use a modem to dial into the access provider's computer in order to then link with the rest of the Internet.

CHAPTER

2

Anatomy of a Web Connection

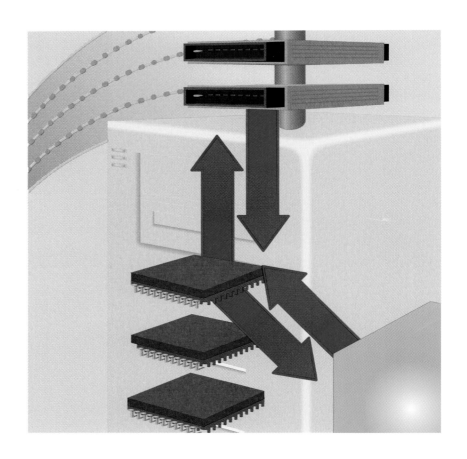

PERHAPS you've had people ask you to help them get "on the Web," a phrase that makes it sound as though the World Wide Web is some kind of cyber-bus and your friends need you to give them a leg up. For beginners, that leg up is probably a basic primer on connecting a desktop computer to any other computer or network of computers via a modem. This chapter is geared toward novices, to help them understand what it takes to get on board.

A home Internet connection consists of four basic parts: the desktop or client computer, the Internet access provider, the host or server computer at the other end of the connection, and the telecommunications networks that link the first three components together. The desktop is the command and control station from which you direct your navigation of the Web. At this starting point of the connection, you need a few basic hardware components (the PC, of course; a fast modem; and a telephone line) and some software (a Web "browser" and an integrated communications program). The browser sends instructions to the communications program to contact a specific computer on the Web and retrieve a specific Web document or page. The communications program dials the modem, which allows the browser to send the request using the Internet's protocol known as TCP/IP (transmission control protocol/Internet protocol). This protocol breaks the request, and the answer to it, into small data packets that are routed across the Internet. Optional components might include a large color monitor, a good sound card, and a dedicated phone line so you can receive calls while you're on the Web. If you're connecting from work, your connection might look somewhat different. A PC on a network can share a modem with other computers on the network, for example, or the business may be directly connected to the Internet, and thus not need to mediate the connection through an Internet provider.

Most individuals working from desktop computers are unable to connect directly to the Internet's backbone network, because they don't have the ultra high-speed telecommunications lines required to link directly to the Internet. To reach the Internet, then, most desktop computers call an intermediary computer at a company that serves as an *Internet access provider*, also known as the Internet service provider, or ISP. The ISP acts as a conduit for individuals to dial in, then be patched through to the Internet backbone.

When viewing Web pages through a browser on a client computer, you typically move among many Web pages and between multiple Web sites. When you make a connection to these sites, you will see the name of the location that houses the pages. This location is called a *domain*. The domain name is located right after the *http://* in any URL. A single domain can house thousands of Web pages. Web users often recall memorable domain names or make educated guesses about where domain names will lead them. If you want to set up your own Web site, you will probably want to register a unique domain name associated with the site.

In the United States, domain names are assigned through an agency called InterNIC. If your business or school has a Web server, chances are it registered a unique domain name with InterNIC. NIC stands for Network Information Centers. InterNIC is a collaborative effort between Network Solutions Inc. (NSI), AT&T, and General Atomics of San Diego, California. NSI provides registration services; AT&T provides directory services; and General Atomics manages information and other services on behalf of the scientific and education community. The counterpart to InterNIC in Europe is RIPE Network Coordination Centre. In the Asian-Pacific region, APNIC handles registration.

You can register your own domain name with InterNIC for a small fee. First, visit the InterNIC Web site (URL: http://www.internic.net). Next, do a search of their database of registered domain names to see if the one you want is available. You should have a highly original name in mind before registering. Any copyright issues are your responsibility, so be sure your domain name is unique. The registration fee is $100 for the first two years and $50 a year thereafter. The administrative costs for registering domain names are funded by the National Science Foundation. Registration fees are a relatively recent development. The explosive growth of the Web has necessitated the fees, and for the time being InterNIC is the only way to register a domain name. In July, 1994, there were 18,000 registered domain names. Exactly one year later InterNIC had 83,000 registered domain names in its database.

The land rush to the Web has made memorable domain names a valuable commodity. Large corporations have already registered names such as "toothpaste.com" and "toiletpaper.com" before even creating a Web presence. However, InterNIC frowns upon stockpiling domain names and later selling them off to companies for a profit.

When a client computer communicates with a domain, the English name must be changed to a numerical scheme called an IP (Internet Protocol) address. If you use your local ISP to serve your personal Web pages, it is possible to register a unique domain name that the ISP assigns to a unique IP address. Names are "resolved" to IP addresses using the Domain Name System, or DNS. The DNS was developed by Sun Microsystems in the early 1980s and is the addressing system on the Internet. There are computers called domain name servers that house tables full of domain names and their corresponding IP addresses. DNS and name servers route clients (that is, Web surfers like you) to the right host computer with the right Web page.

Host computers that are spread throughout the Internet house the data—the Web pages—that you're really after when you get "on the Web." Host computers differ from desktop computers in that they can handle multiple telecommunications connections at one time. Usually, they also have gigabytes of hard-disk storage, considerable random-access memory, and a high-speed processor. In fact, some host systems may actually be several computers linked together with each handling incoming Web page requests.

Weaving these systems together is the world's communications infrastructure, virtually the same telephone lines, fiber optic cables, and satellite links that companies use to send voice calls, pictures, and data from one location to the next. You'll often hear of several types of high-speed connections that make using the Web much more efficient. There are two types of leased lines that provide a fast, dedicated circuit between the computer systems connected to the Internet. They are called *T1* and *T3* lines. These connections range in speed from 1.544 Kbps to as fast as 45 megabits per second. The fastest of these is the T3 line, which is used as the backbone of the Internet connection. T1 lines are generally used by Internet access providers to connect to the computer systems on the backbone.

ISDN, or integrated services digital network, is now available to homes in many areas across the country. ISDN lines are designed to transmit digital information at speeds of 128Kbps, about five times faster than the fastest analog modems used on most desktop computers.

It sounds simple enough, and it is, as the following illustration will demonstrate.

How Web Connections Work

2 Your telecommunications connection follows either the POTS or ISDN line until it reaches the telephone company's central office. The central office routes calls either through its own network of copper, fiber optic, or satellite links, or to a long distance carrier's point of presence, or POP. (The POP is the point at which a local call is handed off to a long distance company.) The call is then routed to the central office nearest the Internet service provider.

1 A fast modem is essential for Web cruising. You may use a 28.8 kilobits-per-second modem that converts digital information from the computer into the analog signals transmitted by ordinary phone lines (sometimes called POTS, or plain old telephone service). ISDN lines are available in some residential areas that transfer digital data at speeds up to 128Kbps.

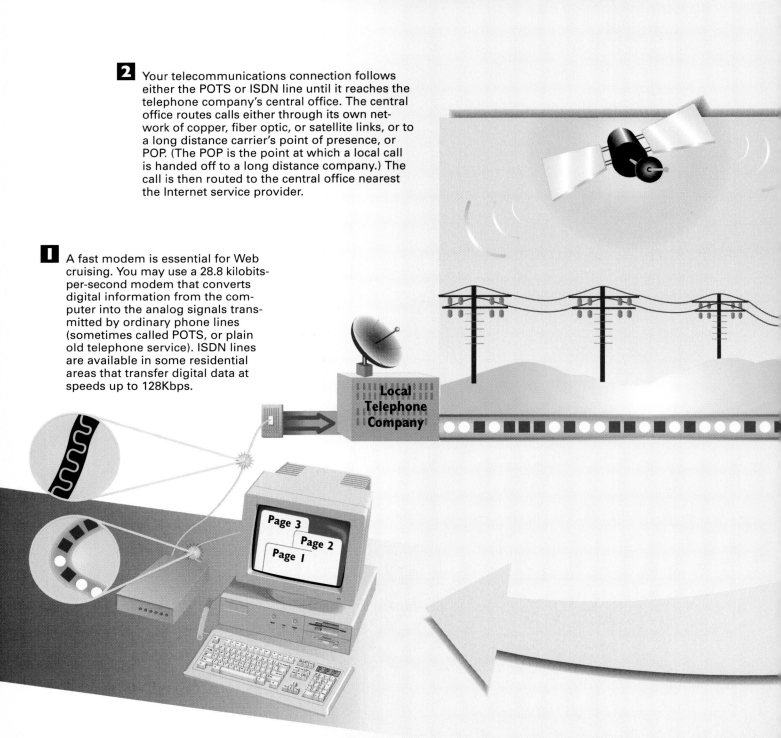

Local
Telephone
Company

Page 3
Page 2
Page 1

3 The ISP receives your incoming call and processes your request, passing the connection to its leased line link to a computer on the Internet backbone, usually a T1 connection. Typically, the ISP has a rack of modems that accepts multiple incoming calls simultaneously. Your connection is complete when it reaches the host computer.

T1

T1

T3

Processors

Response   Requests

Web Software

Page 3

Page 2

Page 1

5 The host also runs special Web server software that reads requests sent from the client computer and retrieves and sends to the client the appropriate information stored on the host. These host computers may have dedicated T1 or T3 links to the Internet backbone, or may be connected to the backbone through a network of hosts.

Long-Distance Telephone Company

4 Computers with dedicated links to the Internet backbone must always be on, and the connection must always be open. These computers are assigned a permanent IP (Internet Protocol) address, which is a multidigit number. This address allows other machines to find it. When you connect to the Internet via an Internet Access Provider, your connection to the Internet backbone is opened and your computer is assigned a temporary IP address.

Web Note

Using an ISP allows subscribers to dial in when it is convenient for them. When subscribers dial in, the ISP assigns a temporary IP address to their computer so they can communicate with the rest of the Internet and the Web.

CHAPTER

3

How a Web Page Works

OFTEN when people talk about the World Wide Web, they use the word *page.* "That's an interesting page," they say, or "What's the address of your page?" The idea stems from the concept of the Web as a collection of published documents, where a document is made up of many pages, just as a book is a collection of pages.

In fact, the Web presents information in "pages" formatted primarily as text and graphics. But it isn't quite accurate to think of a Web page as a sheet of paper or a page from a book with specific bounds of width and height. Rather, think of a Web page as a unit of information. A page can be as long as one or more chapters of a book, for example, or as short as a single word or sentence, much like a word processing document can be very long or rather brief. The size of the page is defined by embedding codes in the document that signify where a page begins and ends. The page is the single unit of information requested and received, then displayed at one time in a browser.

While pages can be any length, for practical purposes they are usually only as long as a word processing document of several printed pages because documents much longer than that can be difficult to read on the computer screen. Of course the typical computer screen can only show about three or four paragraphs at a time. So when you view a Web page in a browser, you often must scroll or page down through the document in order to see the entire page. You may even decide to print the page, in which case your printer is likely to spew out several pages, just as if you were printing a long document from a word processor. In fact, a Web page is not all that different from a word processed document (many Web pages *start out* as word processed documents) that has been embedded with special formatting codes to tell the Web browser how to display the page. (More on that in the next chapter.)

And while we're stretching the bounds of the printed page, let's also remember that a Web page isn't a static set of words and graphics. New multimedia technologies are turning static pages into *active* pages. Real-time audio players let you listen to music, words, and other recordings as you browse a Web site. Server push and more recently Shockwave play animated sequences on the Web page. The Java programming language lets Web site developers embed small applications into Web pages, so that a bank might include a loan calculator on its Web page, for example, enabling you to calculate interest costs while reading about the bank's loan offerings. VRML is bringing "virtual worlds" to the Web, creating three-dimensional spaces that you can pan through and explore. You won't find any of this on a printed page.

In fact, as creative people find more ways to use the Web, the page metaphor is becoming obsolete. In some cases, the Web "page" is a package, bundling together downloadable software programs, other documents, sounds, graphics—just about any type of media you can imagine. In another instance, the Web "page" is more like a window, letting people look into a database, for example, and extract from it the very specific information they were seeking.

These information types and applications go beyond simple Web pages, and deserve a lot more attention than we can give them here. In fact, we've given over the entire Part 3 to discussing these topics. For now, we'll stick to the basic components of a Web page and how pages are organized on a Web site.

The term *home page* is often used to refer to the first, or top, page in a collection of pages that make up a Web *site*—one or more pages collected together as a single "package" of sorts. The home page is like a magazine cover or the front page of a newspaper. This usage is popular, but not quite correct. The "home page" is specific to each user who can set any page on the Web to be the default home page. This default "home page" is retrieved automatically each time the user launches the browser. Browser software companies typically set this default page to be the top or *welcome page* of their Web site, but you are able to change that setting to be any page you prefer. A home page should be a familiar starting place from which you begin each Web exploration. Most browsers have a "home" icon that when selected retrieves this starting page, no matter where else you've wandered on the Web. Of course, as more Web explorers use the words "home page" to describe the introductory page of a site, the difference between a home page and a welcome page may become moot.

For the sake of correctness, at least for the time being, we'll use the term *welcome page* to mean the entry point of a Web site. Usually, the welcome page acts as an introduction to a Web site, explaining the purpose of a site and describing the information found on other pages throughout the site. In this way, the welcome page also often acts as the table of contents for the rest of the site, providing the connections from the top page to other pages throughout the site.

So, for example, if this book were a Web site, the Introduction, and perhaps a graphic image of the cover, would be the first thing you saw when you accessed the site; it would serve as a welcome page. If you scrolled down the welcome page, the Table of Contents would outline the information found on this How the World Wide Web Works site. Furthermore, if you were to set your browser so that you always accessed the How the World Wide Web Works welcome page first when you connected to the Web, that page could also be your home page. After you read the Introduction and scanned the table of contents, you could click on "Chapter 3: How a Web Page Works" to connect you to the Web page that contained the text of this chapter.

The concept of a Web page is relatively simple and is probably best understood graphically. Turn the page to see what we mean.

How Pages Are Organized on a Web Site

A Web site is one or many pages of information linked together in a single package. Web sites can be organized very simply, in a hierarchy that progresses from general to specific information; or they can be complex, with pages that seem to link randomly to other pages on the site (see the opposite page).

1 The *welcome page* is the first or top page of any Web site. A site can be just one page, or can comprise dozens or even hundreds of pages. In the latter case, the welcome page acts as a table of contents to organize the site and help users find information available on the site.

2 Underlined or highlighted hyperlink text is often embedded in the welcome page. The hyperlinks serve to connect the top page with other pages throughout the site.

3 Related documents residing together on a Web host computer make up a Web site. However, a single server can host multiple Web sites, each contained in a separate area or directory, much like a hard drive can accommodate multiple directories.

4 Good Web design principles suggest that pages throughout a site link back to the welcome page. This approach allows users to always find their way back to the top of a site in order to navigate in other directions.

5 Documents within a site can be linked to any other document in the site—and even to documents on other sites. Most Web sites, however, are designed in a pyramid or outline structure that gives users a visual model to understand how information is arranged, and indicates how to find and navigate through the site's documents.

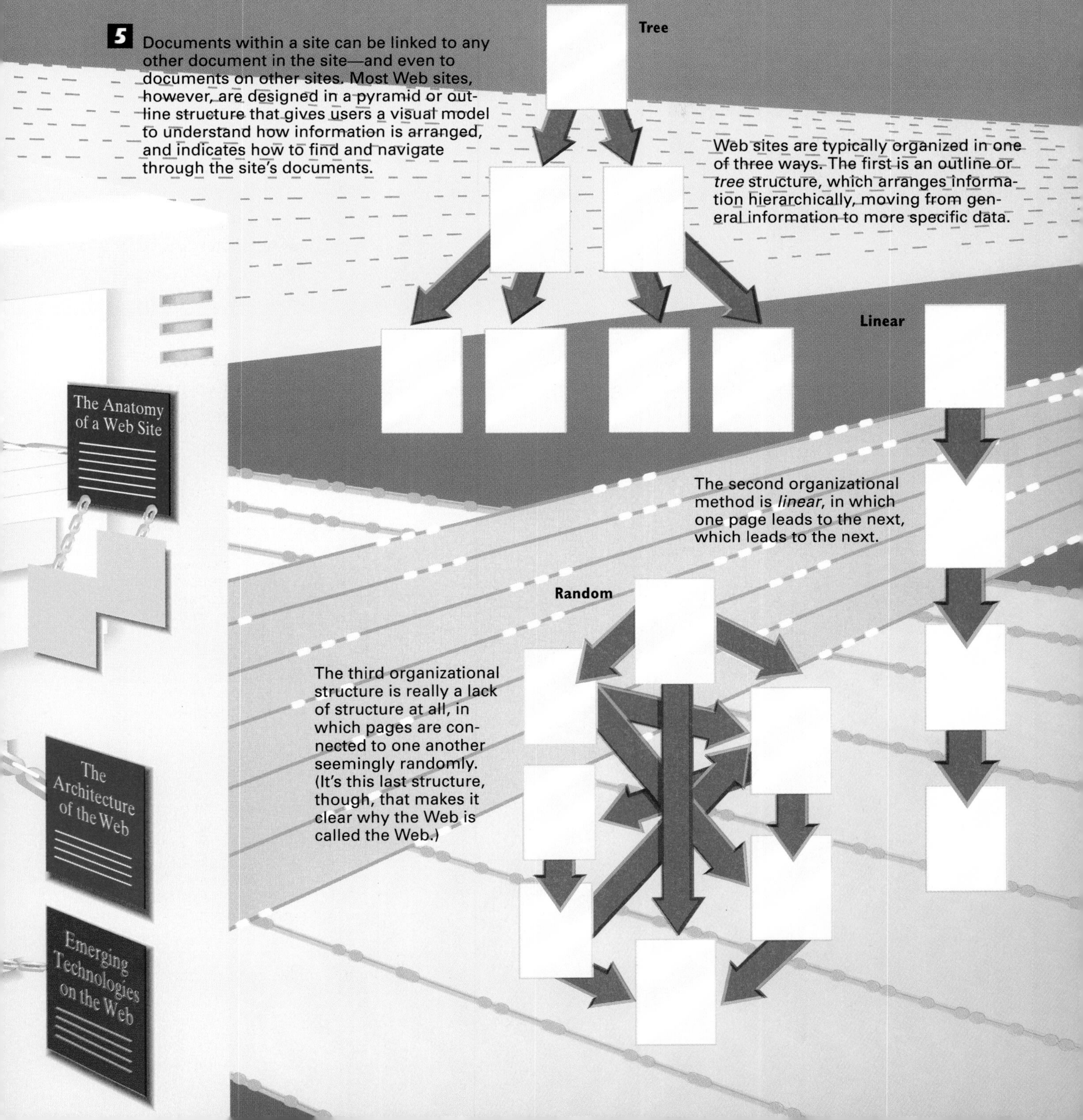

Tree

Web sites are typically organized in one of three ways. The first is an outline or *tree* structure, which arranges information hierarchically, moving from general information to more specific data.

Linear

The second organizational method is *linear*, in which one page leads to the next, which leads to the next.

Random

The third organizational structure is really a lack of structure at all, in which pages are connected to one another seemingly randomly. (It's this last structure, though, that makes it clear why the Web is called the Web.)

The Anatomy of a Web Site

The Architecture of the Web

Emerging Technologies on the Web

CHAPTER

4

How Markup Languages Work

MARKUP

MARKUP languages are the building blocks of a Web page. They are sets of directions that tell the browser software how to display and manage a Web document, much like written music scores are instructions that tell a musician how to play a particular song. These instructions, or markups, are embedded in the content of the source document to create the Web page. The markup also references graphic images located in separate files, and instructs the browser to retrieve and display these images within the text page. This makes each Web page portable because it has everything it needs to be displayed appropriately on any computer and by any browser that can interpret the markup language. It is this concept that gives the Web the "World Wide" part of its moniker. Again, like music, markup languages are the closest means of universal data sharing that is currently possible.

Markup languages should not be confused with programming codes like C+ or Pascal. Rather, markups consist of data that is embedded within existing documents to describe how they should be formatted. There are four types of markup: descriptive markup (or "tags"), references, declarations, and processing instructions. Details of page layout (such as fonts and point sizes) are not a part of a markup language's instructions; the browser determines these features. Markups of existing data do not change the data, nor do they determine the exact layout of a Web page. Instead, a markup language provides a general structure of headings, paragraphs, images, and so on. It is up to the individual browser to specify how each structural level of a document will be displayed.

Hypertext markup language (HTML) is the specific markup language of the Web. It defines the format of a Web document and enables hypertext links to be embedded in the document (see Chapter 5 for a complete discussion of hypertext). You can use any text editor or word processor to add HTML markups to an ASCII text document. The language and its instructions can be easily learned and memorized. You don't have to be a genius computer hacker to grasp the concept or the specific usage of HTML. In fact, there are a number of shareware and commercially available HTML editors that assist Web page authors in incorporating HTML tags into a document. Most HTML editors provide lists of tags and instructions that you can select by pointing to and clicking on them.

HTML is an implementation of *standard generalized markup language* (SGML), a more sophisticated and complex markup language. HTML remains simple because its primary task is to allow text to link to other pages on the Web. For example, say you want to write a Web page that highlights your interest in sailing. You would use HTML to mark up the word "boating" in your list of hobbies in order to create a hyperlink from the word "boating" to another site on the Web that deals with sailing.

Perhaps the best way to get a feel for HTML is to look at the difference between plain text, created in an ordinary word processor, and text that is "marked up" using HTML. Let's work with the boating example just mentioned. An excerpt from the plain text document would look like this:

Let me tell you about a few of my **hobbies**. I have enjoyed boating since I was a young boy when I sailed each summer on Lake Michigan. My interest in sailing led to other hobbies, my favorite of which is astronomy.

Now, let's look at that paragraph "marked up" in HTML and ready to be displayed as a Web page:

```
<p>
Let me tell you about a few of my <B>hobbies</B>. I have enjoyed <A
HREF="http://www.sail.com/">boating</A> since I was a young boy when I sailed
each summer on Lake Michigan. My interest in sailing led to other hobbies, my favorite
of which is <A HREF="http://www.stars.com/">astronomy</A>.
```

The HTML tag <B> and </B> tells a browser to display the word or words, in this case "hobbies," between the two tags in bold. The tag <A HREF= tells the browser to create a link to the Web page referenced by the URL indicated in quotation marks and to use the word or words between the > character and the </A> tag as the hyperlinked word or words, in this case "boating" and later in the paragraph "astronomy."

There is another language on the Web whose presence is steadily increasing. *Virtual reality modeling language* (VRML) is a highly complex modeling language used to display three-dimensional, interactive environments. VRML is not a markup language, however, many of the developers of VRML are on the cutting edge of Web technology, and some even peg VRML as the wave of the future because it enables Web developers to create sites that the user can explore by scrolling around the page. The effect is similar to walking into a room and looking around at everything in the room. The basic function of the language is akin to HTML in that both provide universal instructions to Web browsers, and both determine the basic formatting rules for display of the information. VRML, however, must give instructions about how to render three-dimensional moving objects, which takes many times more instruction lines, much more computer processing power, and much faster modems to send this large amount of data from the Web site to the client PC. (For an in-depth look at VRML, turn to Chapter 19.)

Just as the Web evolves daily, HTML expands and changes. To keep pace with this growth, a group of Web engineers and designers—called the World Wide Web Consortium, or W3C—

is currently in charge of updating HTML specifications and producing reference software. The HTML 3.0 reference is called Arena, and was set by the Internet Engineering Task Force (IETF), a volunteer body assembled by W3 to evaluate and set standards for HTML. You can find the latest developments of the Consortium by checking into their Web page at http://www.w3.org/hypertext/WWW/TheProject/.

But even while this body slowly builds consensus and develops HTML standards, others are creating and using tags that are outside the standards. These companies, such as Netscape, create new, nonstandard tags that expand the power of HTML but reduce its portability. As a result, you need specific browsers in order to properly display a page that uses these nonstandard tags—at least until these new tags are incorporated into the next HTML standards reference. This process of creating standards, then pushing beyond them is what keeps HTML a vibrant and constantly improving markup language for the Web.

How HTML Works

HTML is an instruction set that is embedded in all Web documents. Your original text will probably have headings, multiple paragraphs, and some simple formatting. A Web browser will not understand all of these layout instructions. Paragraphs, carriage returns, indents, and multiple spaces will instead be shown as a single space if no HTML markup is added.

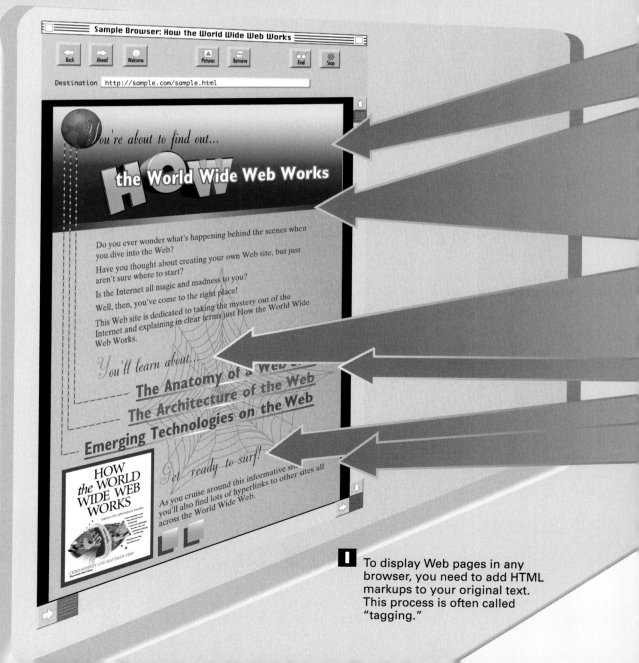

1 To display Web pages in any browser, you need to add HTML markups to your original text. This process is often called "tagging."

2 Use HTML to give your text structure. All HTML files begin and end with the HTML tags. Headings are marked as such, as are paragraphs, line breaks, block quotes, and special character emphasis. Any carriage returns or indentations within the source text are simply to improve readability. They in no way affect the browser's display of the page.

3 The finished HTML document will be the source page for any browser on any computer. The simplicity of HTML makes cross-platform compatibility easy and reliable. Yet the more complex and specialized the HTML tagging is, the longer it will take to download and display.

Display text "How the World Wide Web Works"

```
<HTML>
<HEAD>
<TITLE>Sample Browser: How The World Wide Web Works</TITLE>
</HEAD>
```

```
<BODY background= "Spider.GIF">
<IMG SRC = "top.gif">
<P>
<BLOCKQUOTE>
Do you ever wonder what's happening behind the scenes when you dive into the Web?
<P>
Have you thought about creating your own Web site, but just aren't sure where to start?
<P>
Is the Internet all magic and madness to you?
<P>
Well, then, you've come to the right place!
<P>
This web site is dedicated to taking the mystery out of the Internet and explaining in clear terms just How the World Wide Web Works.
```

Display text "Do you ever wonder..."

```
<H1> You'll learn about...</H1>
<BLOCKQUOTE>
<A HREF = "anatomy.html">The Anatomy of a Web Site</A>
<P>
<A HREF = "architecture.html">The Architecture of the Web</A>
<P>
<A HREF = "emerging.html">Emerging Technologies on the Web</A>
</BLOCKQUOTE>
</BLOCKQUOTE>
```

Display text "You'll learn about. . ."

```
<IMG SRC = "footer.gif" ALIGN=LEFT>
```

Create a link to this site

```
<BLOCKQUOTE>
<H2> Get ready to surf!</H2>
```

Display text "Get ready to surf!"

```
As you cruise around this informative site, you'll also find lots of hyperlinks to other sites all across the World Wide Web.
</BLOCKQUOTE>
```

Display text "As you cruise..."

```
</BODY>
</HTML>
```

4 Most Web browsers will allow your document to retain its structural integrity when you display, or "parse," it. However, the look may vary from browser to browser. For example, headings will appear in a larger font size than text within paragraphs, and block quotes will be uniformly indented. Note that browsers determine exact font, size, and color. However, the relative importance of the elements is always kept intact.

CHAPTER
5

How Hypertext Works

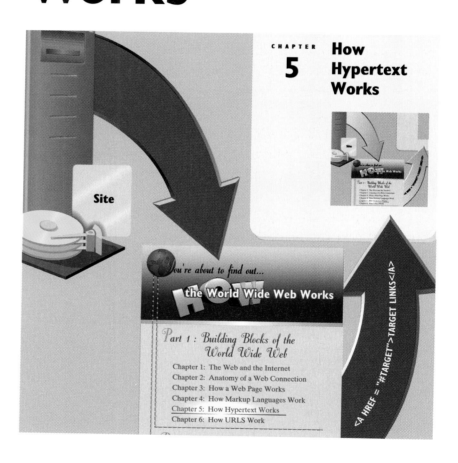

IN the late 1960s, a computer scientist named Ted Nelson introduced "hypertext," a concept that lays the foundation for the World Wide Web and its connections between documents, or pages. At the time, the concept of hypertext documents was revolutionary. Today, it's part and parcel of many multimedia programs, such as encyclopedias on CD-ROM or even interactive entertainment titles, and it is an integral part of the World Wide Web.

Nelson's idea grew from his desire to create a new way of exploring information. He wanted to provide the reader with a spontaneous means of accessing more and more in-depth information about something that sparked the reader's interest when reading text on the page. Rather than reading a document from beginning to end, digesting the material in a sequential order, the reader could highlight a word and receive more information on the meaning of that word, for example. Nelson imagined that you could read the United States Constitution, come across the term "electoral college," and then open another document that explained how the electoral college works. From that document, you might open another document that listed the votes of the electoral college from its founding to the present. From there, you might choose to open a document about William Jefferson Clinton, then another about the First Cat, Socks, then another about the care and feeding of felines, and so forth. Ultimately, you could find yourself a subject that isn't even remotely connected to the Constitution, but which you find interesting or entertaining.

This hypertext concept was obviously on Tim Berners-Lee's mind when he began thinking about how researchers could share their work across the Internet. He envisioned a system where a document could be linked to other documents, enabling researchers to easily find more and related information simply by following a link from one document on the network to another document. (For a little history on the Web, see Chapter 1.)

Typically, hypertext consists of a hyperlink that appears onscreen as a highlighted word, icon, or graphic. By moving a mouse cursor over the item, or object, and clicking on it, you easily navigate to additional information. On the Web, that information can be located at any other place on the Web, be it on the same host server or one across the globe. A linked object can be various media, such as text (linking from one character to a whole document, for example), a graphical button (such as direction arrows that move from page to page), or still images (photos, icons, or a comic strip), for example.

A hypertext document can be linked to other information on the Web in one of three ways:

First, a word or phrase can be linked to another section within the same Web page. The destinations arrived at by clicking on these links may be called local targets, or simply *targets*.

Many pages list the contents of the page at the top of the document. By selecting an item from the list, you navigate quickly to that section of the document. So, for example, if this book were presented as one very, very long Web page, the table of contents would be listed at the top of the document. By selecting "Chapter 5: How Hypertext Works" from the table of contents listing, your Web browser would move directly to the section of the document that contained the section that is Chapter 5.

Second, Web pages link to pages within the current site. A *relative link* is one that is forward or backward relative to the current page. For example, if this book were a Web site, each chapter could be a page on the site. Any time a reference to another chapter was made in the text, you could navigate to that chapter's page using only its name rather than its full URL. That's because that page is part of the same site as the page you are currently viewing; it is *relative* to the current page. For instance, if a reference to "Chapter 2" appeared in the text, you would be able to link directly to the page that contains the text of Chapter 2.

The third way Web pages are linked is from one site to another, often called an *external* or *absolute* link. This is not much different from a link within a site, except that it enables the author of a Web site to link documents he or she creates to those stored on a host elsewhere on the World Wide Web.

If you can imagine these links tying sites together all over the world, you will begin to see why this collection of documents on the Internet is known as the World Wide *Web*. The links from document to document can get quite tangled up. If it were possible to make a diagram of them, they would look a great deal like an intricate spider's web.

Hypertext links are embedded into a Web document using the hypertext markup language. (For more on HTML, see Chapter 4.) A text link usually appears on the screen as an underlined word or phrase, and is sometimes rendered in a different color from other text, depending on how your Web browser interprets the HTML codes. When you place the mouse cursor on this underlined text and click the mouse button, you initiate a request by the browser for a new Web page or—if the text references an *internal* link to information in the same document—direct your browser to scroll to another, specific point within the same document.

In addition to text, images or icons can also act as hyperlinks. When you move the mouse cursor over the icon or graphic and click the mouse button, you launch the request to retrieve the linked information.

While it's not our intention to teach HTML programming in this book, a look at the HTML code for a link demonstrates how this linking system works. Typically, a hypertext link will look like this:

> Please turn to <A HREF="../chap5/index.html">Chapter 5: How Hypertext Works</A> to learn more about hypertext.

(You would use the full URL—<A HREF="http://www.server.com/book/Chap5/index.html/"> if the document is located on another Web site.) In this instance, you might be reading a summary Web page about this book and see text that looks like this:

> Please turn to <u>Chapter 5: How Hypertext Works</u> to learn more about hypertext.

Clicking on the underlined text would cause the browser to request the Chapter 5 Web page from the How the World Wide Web Works site. That new page would then be displayed when it is loaded into the browser.

A graphic link, say one in which an icon was used as the anchor for a hyperlink, would look like this in HTML:

> When you see this symbol, click on it to return to the table of contents.
> <a href="../TOC/index.htm/"><img src="/zdpress/gifs/toc.jpg"></a>

The Web page parsed from that code might look like this:

> When you see this symbol, click on it to return to the table of contents. **TOC**

By clicking on the icon, you instruct the browser to retrieve the Web page that contains the Table of Contents.

How Hyperlinks Work

Hyperlinks are used to navigate within a document, or from one document to another, on the Web. An HTML command embedded in a document creates the *anchor* of a hyperlink. The anchor points to a *destination* location. In HTML parlance, a link's destination is surrounded by anchor tags, which provide directions to the destination page. There are three types of hyperlinks: target links, relative links, and absolute links.

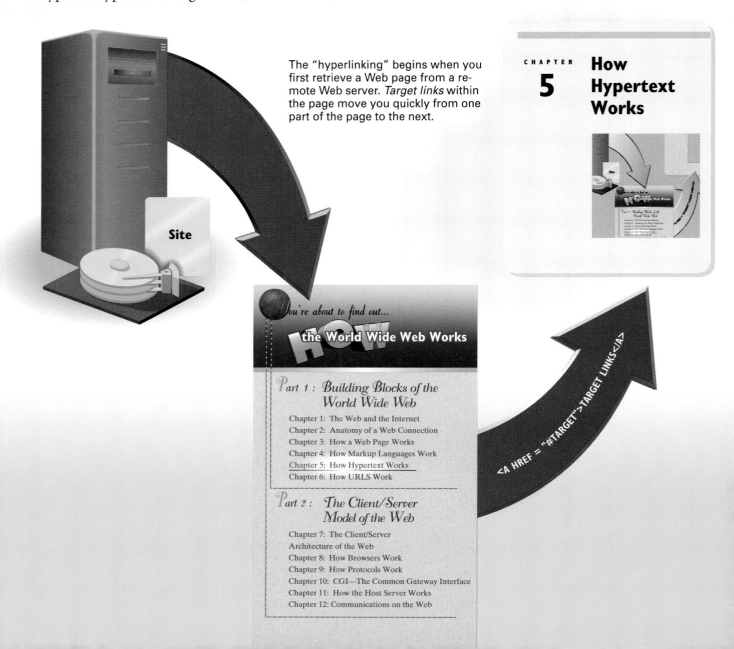

The "hyperlinking" begins when you first retrieve a Web page from a remote Web server. *Target links* within the page move you quickly from one part of the page to the next.

CHAPTER

5

How Hypertext Works

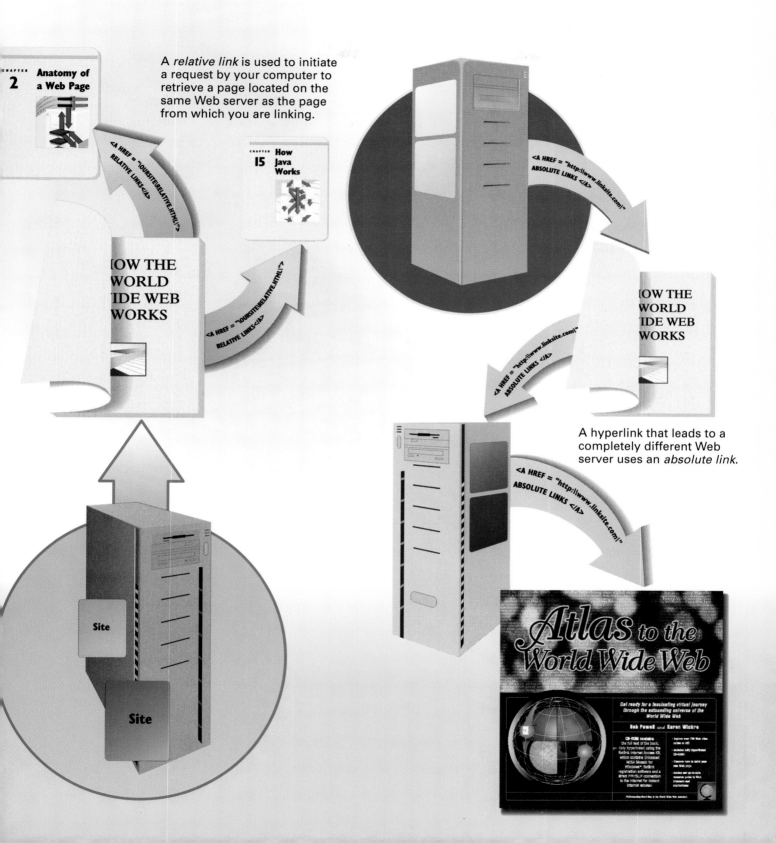

A *relative link* is used to initiate a request by your computer to retrieve a page located on the same Web server as the page from which you are linking.

<A HREF = "/OURSITE/RELATIVE.HTML">
RELATIVE LINKS</A>

<A HREF = "/OURSITE/RELATIVE.HTML">
RELATIVE LINKS</A>

<A HREF = "http://www.linksite.com/"
ABSOLUTE LINKS </A>

<A HREF = "http://www.linksite.com/"
ABSOLUTE LINKS </A>

<A HREF = "http://www.linksite.com/"
ABSOLUTE LINKS </A>

A hyperlink that leads to a completely different Web server uses an *absolute link*.

CHAPTER 2 Anatomy of a Web Page

CHAPTER 15 How Java Works

HOW THE WORLD WIDE WEB WORKS

HOW THE WORLD WIDE WEB WORKS

Site

Site

CHAPTER 6

How URLs Work

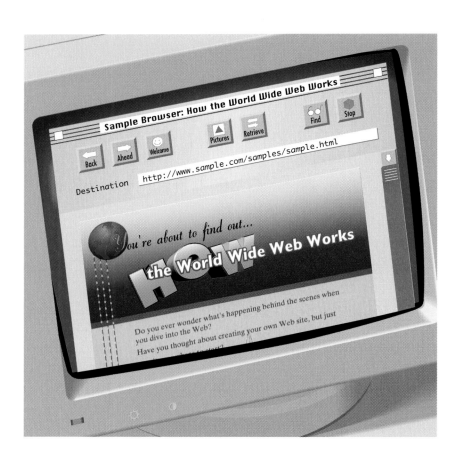

WEB pages reside on host computers located throughout the Internet. The Web pages and the hosts must both be uniquely identified so that your computer can locate and retrieve the pages. The unique identifier for a host is called the IP (Internet Protocol) address, and the unique identifier for a page is called the URL, or uniform resource locator. This acronym is sometimes pronounced as "earl." The pronounced acronym is gaining acceptance in some quarters, but you are still more likely to hear URL spelled out (U-R-L) or referred to as the *address*. In fact, a URL functions much like a postal or electronic-mail (e-mail) address. Just as postal and e-mail addresses list a name and specific location, a URL, or Web address, indicates where the host computer is located, the location of the Web site on the host, and the name of the Web page and the file type of each document, among other information. The key difference between a postal or e-mail address, however, is that a Web address is a point of retrieval, not a final destination.

A typical URL looks like this:

```
http://www.zdpress.com/webworks/index.html/
```

If you were to interpret the instructions in this URL from left to right, it would translate to: "Go to the host computer called *zdpress* (a commercial business), in a directory called *webworks*, and retrieve a hypertext document with the file name *index.html*." The URL, or address, tells the browser what document to fetch and exactly where to find it on a specific remote host computer somewhere on the Internet.

The first part of the URL indicates what type of transfer protocol will be used to retrieve the specified document. The most common request is for a hypertext document that uses *http* (Hypertext Transfer Protocol).

The second portion of the URL refers to the specific host computer on which the document resides and that is to be contacted by the browser software. This part of the address is also called the *domain* name. The broadest level of a domain name is the suffix that indicates what kind of organization the domain is. For example, *.com* indicates a commercial business, *.edu* indicates a college or university, *.gov* indicates a government office, *.mil* a military facility, and *.org* a not-for-profit organization. The suffix can also indicate the country in which the host computer is located. For example, *.ca* is in Canada and *.au* is in Australia. As you move to the left, the names become more specific and resolve to a smaller group of addresses. These groups are called *sub-domains*. So *.zdpress* is a subdomain of the domain *.com*, and *www* is a subdomain of the server called *zdpress*.

It is important here, though, to clarify the difference between an IP address and a domain name. Every computer on the Internet has a unique IP address. An IP address is made up of a series of numbers, and is usually expressed as a dotted decimal number that looks like this:

155.40.200.45.

Unfortunately, human beings have a difficult time remembering long strings of numbers. That is where domain names come in. A domain name is a unique word that acts as a nickname of sorts for the IP address. So, instead of having to enter a long numeric string into the URL, you can simply enter the host server's unique domain name.

The third part of the URL is the directory on the host computer that contains a specific Web site or multiple Web sites. This is always located after the first single slash in the URL, and is essentially the subdirectory on the hard disk that houses the Web site. Subdirectories might also be indicated in this part of the address. For example, if the above URL was changed to:

http://www.zdpress.com/webworks/partone/chapters/chapte.html

then there are two subdirectories—*partone* and *chapters.*

In the above example, the file name is *chapte.html.* This is always the last portion of the URL. If you see an address without a file name, it is assumed that the file name *index.html* contains the requested Web page. The default document a Web server will deliver to the client when no other file name is listed is index.html. Even though a Web address may not list a file name, there is always a file name at the end of all URLs. In these cases, the file name *index.html* is implied.

The illustration in this chapter shows the process necessary to request and retrieve a Web document. When a request for a document occurs for the first time in a Web-browsing session, the host computer must first be located in order to find the file. If the URL contained the host computer's IP address, the page request could travel directly to the host computer. Because most URLs use the domain name, a process called *domain name resolution* or simply *name resolution* is needed to find the host computer.

When a domain name is resolved, it is simply being translated into a unique all-number IP address that all computers on the Internet can recognize. Actual name resolution takes place on the Internet on computers called *domain name servers* (DNSs). Name servers have automated programs that translate domain names into IP address numbers. Such machines are accessed by smaller servers on the Net many times per second. And if one name server does not know how to translate a domain name into an IP address, the task will be sent to the next closest name server, all within milliseconds.

One way to imagine this process in the physical world is with zip codes. Say you take a letter with a correct address and no zip code to your local post office. The postal worker looks at a chart of zip codes or consults a computer database, finds the correct zip code, and then writes the code on your letter. The zip code vastly speeds delivery; plus, you only had to remember the city and state, not a long code of numbers.

The Structure of a URL

The URL tells the browser what document to fetch and exactly where to find it on a remote host computer somewhere on the Internet.

1 The first part of the URL indicates what type of transfer protocol will be used to retrieve the specified document. The most common request is for a hypertext document that uses the http protocol.

3 The third part of the URL is the directory on the host computer that contains a specific Web site. A host computer can house multiple Web sites. This third segment of the address is essentially the root directory that houses the site. Subdirectories might also be indicated in this part of the address.

Back   Ahead   Welcome   Pictures   Retrieve   Find   Stop

Destination `http://www.sample.com/samples/sample.html`

2 The second portion of the URL is the specific host computer on which the document resides and that is to be contacted by the browser software. This part of the address is also called the *domain*. Domain names end in a suffix that indicates what kind of organization the domain is. For example, *.com* indicates a commercial business, *.edu* indicates a college or university, *.gov* indicates a government office, *.mil* a military facility, and *.org* a not-for-profit organization. The suffix can also indicate the country in which the host computer is located. For example, *.ca* is in Canada and *.au* is in Australia.

4 The last segment of the URL is the file name of the specific Web page you are requestion. If no file name is indicated, the browser will assume a default page, usually called index.html.

How URLs Help Retrieve Web Documents

When you enter a URL in your browser software or click on a hyperlink on a Web page, the browser software reads the URL and interprets its parts, as if reading a map, determining the host and the specific document to be retrieved.

1 The Web browser installed on your local computer sends your TCP/IP software a signal that it is ready to request a document. TCP/IP makes a connection with the host TCP/IP software. Once the connection is established, your browser makes a request for a document by sending its URL through the two-way connection maintained by TCP/IP to the server.

2 The HTTP server is the portion of the host computer that runs http-server software. TCP/IP makes and maintains the connection between the client and the host. In this way, the browser can use HTTP to send requests and receive pages through the host's Web server software. This software allows the host to communicate with the client browser, in HTTP, over TCP/IP.

3 The server then receives the transmitted URL and responds in one of three ways: It follows the directory path given in the URL, the server finds the file on its local hard disk and opens it, the server runs a CGI script (see Chapter 10), or it detects an error (such as "file not found") and generates an error document to be sent back to the client.

Document File Type? x-html

5 The browser on your local computer reads the file type. If it is an HTML document, the browser examines the content, breaking it down into meaningful parts. Two general parts include text, which is displayed by the browser word for word; the other part consists of HTML markup information called tags that are not displayed, but display formatting information, such as normal text, bold headers, or colored hypertext. The results are displayed on your monitor.

4 If the document is found, the host checks its file type (usually either x-html or x-text) and sends this information to the client with the requested page. When the client receives the page, it first checks the file type. If the type is one it can display it does so, otherwise it prompts the user to see if they would like to save it to disk or open it using a helper application. The x-html file type is by far the most common one used when transmitting Web pages.

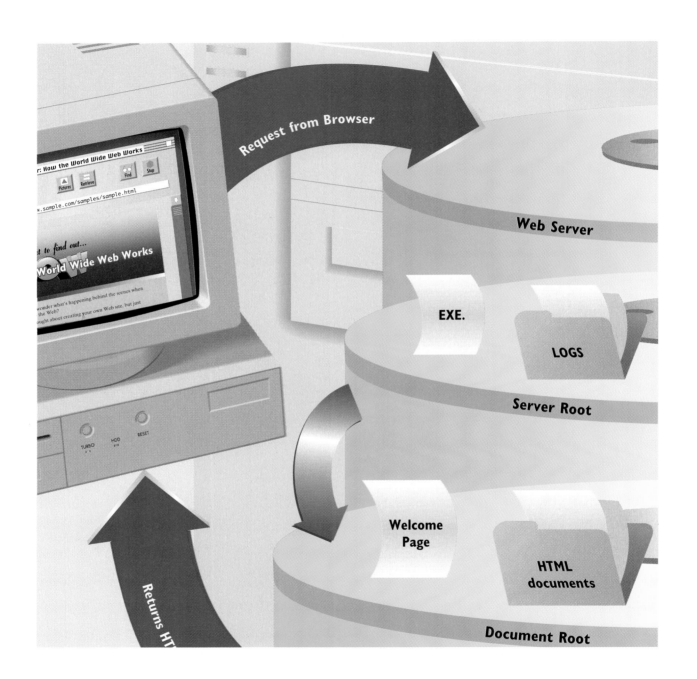

P A R T

THE CLIENT/SERVER MODEL OF THE WEB

THE World Wide Web is a collection of documents that relies on the Internet for delivery. The Web is distributed across the thousands of host computers that tap into the system's communications network. Like other distributed applications, the Web is based on the *client/server* model, in which Web pages reside on host computers that "serve up" pages when a local computer, or client, requests them. Conceptually, the model is simple, although a lot of telecommunications protocols and software engineering go into making it all work.

In simple terms, the person seeking information sits on the client side of the Web connection. The client computer runs the browser software, which asks for specific information by sending an HTTP request across the connection to the host computer. The host computer is on the server end of the connection; the host runs the Web server software. When the server receives the HTTP request, it responds by sending data back to the client.

There are a number of data types that the server can send to the client, and they are distinguished by the Multimedia Internet Mail Extensions (MIME) protocol. There are a number of MIME content types, such as text/html for text formatting, and image/gif and image/jpeg for interpreting graphics. When the browser receives data, it interprets the MIME type and acts on the data accordingly. So in the case of an HTML page, for example, the browser "reads" the tags in the document and formats the document so that it is properly displayed on the screen.

Because this processing happens on the client side of the connection, the server is free to act upon other requests coming in through other clients. Moreover, except for its Internet address, the server doesn't have to know much about the client computer. Because there is no interaction beyond simple HTTP requests and responses, clients and servers can easily run different operating systems, for example, and yet still work together.

It's not absolutely necessary to understand all the nitty-gritty technical pieces of the Web, but it is important to grasp the concept of the client, the server, and the communications protocols in between. This will help you to understand how Web documents traverse the Internet as your request for a page makes its way from your browser (or client) software to a host (or server), is fulfilled, and the Web document is returned to the browser.

Moreover, by distinguishing the client or browser side of the connection from the host or server side, you will come to understand how the Web works for the user as well as the builder of a Web site. In these next few chapters, we'll outline both sides—client and server—of the connection, as well as the communications systems that bring them both together.

CHAPTER

7

The Client/Server Architecture of the Web

THE Web works on the client/server model of information delivery. In this model, a *client* computer connects to a *server* computer on which information resides; the client depends on the server to deliver information. In effect, the client requests the services of the larger computer—usually to search for information and send it back to the client. Typically, the client is a local personal computer, the server (also known as the host) is usually a more powerful computer that houses the data. The connection is via a local area network, a phone line, or a TCP/IP-based wide area network on the Internet. The primary reason to set up a client/server network is to allow many clients to access the same applications and files that are stored on a server.

In the case of the Web, the client is actually the browser on your PC and the server is a host computer located somewhere on the Internet. The browser sends a request (most often a request for a specific Web page) to the server. The server processes that request and sends an answer back to the browser (again, most often in the form of a Web page). And just as a relationship between a client and an attorney, for example, lasts so long as there is business between them, the connection between client and server is maintained only while the exchange of information is being transacted. Thus, after a Web page is transferred from the host (or server) computer, the HTTP connection between that computer and the client is broken. Even though the HTTP connection is closed, the TCP/IP connection to the Internet is maintained via an ISP.

The client/server model enables the desktop PC to run the browser software to search the Web, yet still access host servers around the Internet to execute search and retrieval functions. In essence, this architecture enables the Web to be conceived of as a limitless file storage medium and database, distributed among thousands of host computers, all accessible by any individual PC.

How Client/Server Architecture Works

Client/server systems divide the functions of an application between a local (or client) computer and a connected host (or server) computer.

The PC-based browser software controls the client end of the Web application. Using TCP/IP, the browser issues HTTP requests to the host server. The browser can request a specific Web page, or it can ask the host server to perform a database query. In either instance, the request is broken into HTTP packets sent across the Internet's TCP/IP communications infrastructure to the host computer.

The host computer runs the server software that enables the host to separate the actual request from the packets and perform the asked-for services—either retrieving and sending back to the client PC the specified Web page, or executing a database search and sending the result (in the form of a Web page) back to the client.

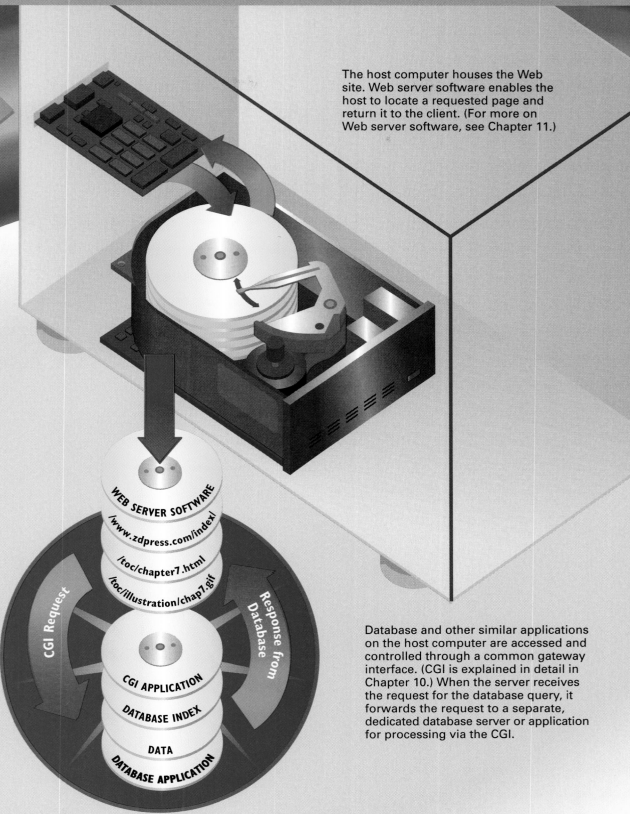

The host computer houses the Web site. Web server software enables the host to locate a requested page and return it to the client. (For more on Web server software, see Chapter 11.)

WEB SERVER SOFTWARE

/www.zdpress.com/index/

/toc/chapter7.html

/toc/illustration/chap7.gif

CGI Request

Response from Database

CGI APPLICATION

DATABASE INDEX

DATA

DATABASE APPLICATION

Database and other similar applications on the host computer are accessed and controlled through a common gateway interface. (CGI is explained in detail in Chapter 10.) When the server receives the request for the database query, it forwards the request to a separate, dedicated database server or application for processing via the CGI.

CHAPTER

8

How Browsers Work

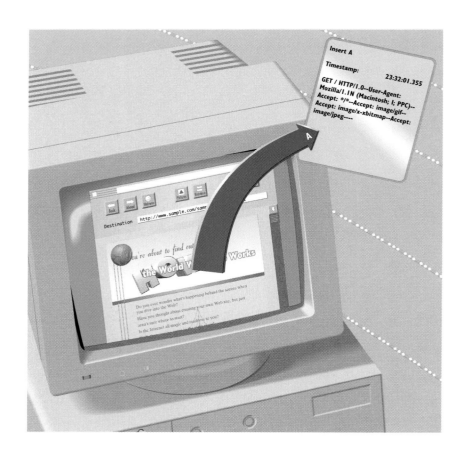

A browser is your window to the World Wide Web. Even with all the hyperlinks, protocols, servers, media, and hypermedia in the world, the Web would be nothing without a browser to put the parts together for you. Your browser is simply a piece of software that coordinates and organizes information, like a word processor for the Web. This "Web processor" is your board as you surf the Web, your RV when you cruise the information superhighway. Whatever travel metaphor you like, the browser is your vehicle.

Today's browsers commonly feature GUIs (graphical user interfaces), which means they use pictures, buttons, and pull-down menus to operate the program. Not true of the "early" Web of the late eighties. Back then you had text-based browsers and Web pages without all of the colorful pages and hypermedia you see today. The first graphical browser, Mosaic, was put together by Marc Andreessen and others at the National Center for Supercomputing Applications (NCSA) in Illinois. Both NCSA Mosaic and Netscape Navigator (the browser Andreessen went on to develop at Netscape) have helped set the standard for the functions and features that most browsers aspire to.

In addition to these two browsers, Microsoft offers the Internet Explorer browser as part of Windows 95. Apple sells the Internet Starter Kit, including a Web browser. And dozens of companies are producing browsers, either as stand-alone products or as part of Internet starter packages. This flood of browser software may sound like a problem for consumers looking to jump on the Web, but most will find their browser software as an extension to their online service, such as America Online or CompuServe, or as part of the bundled software provided by the Internet access service they choose.

A few features are common to most Web browsers. All use basically similar user-interafce designs. They all have menus and icons across the top, along with a data entry field to supply the URL you want the browser to retrieve. Navigation buttons guide you through cyberspace in a linear fashion, either a page forward or a page backward at a time. Pull-down menus provide a history of where you've been during a session on the Web, so you can revisit pages without flipping back through them one by one. Browsers usually offer a "stop" button that when clicked cancels a loading page. Graphics affect the loading time of a page, so look for the option to turn off autoloading of images if you have a slow connection.

Bookmarks are another indispensable feature of most browsers. A bookmark holds your favorite URLs in a list that can be categorized like a directory tree. Think of this list as a virtual bookcase. Favorite sites and frequently used reference materials (such as a hypertext dictionary) go nicely on a bookmark list.

Most browsers will also enable you to set a default home page, that is, the first page automatically loads each time you launch your browser.

Web browsers usually store the text and graphics of recently visited pages into a temporary cache on your hard drive or in RAM. When you quit the browser, the Web pages saved to RAM or written to a hard-drive cache are lost, unless you've directed the browser to save those pages to disk storage. This feature allows fast reload times for pages you've already seen during a Web session, because pages are loaded from your computer rather than transferred over the Internet each time. Hence the first time you load a Web page during a session it will usually take longer than subsequent "visits" to the site.

All browsers support Hypertext Transfer Protocol, or HTTP. (Some full-featured ones also support FTP, EMAIL, NEWS, GOPHER, and SMTP and other MIME types. Support of other protocols is a real benefit because you have the ease-of-use that the Web browser's interface offers while still retrieving and sending documents across the rest of the Internet.) When you enter URLs manually or click on hyperlinks, the browser locates the computer that houses the Web document, then it uses HTTP or another protocol to request the document and download it onto your computer.

After your browser receives data from a server it translates the information into text, hyperlinks, and pictures. The transformation from raw HTML text to a beautifully displayed Web page may seem like magic, but it's not. The browser simply interprets the page format from the embedded HTML tags. For instance, headings are displayed in a relatively larger font than paragraphs, and words with special emphasis are shown with special character formatting such as italics or bold face. This process of reading a page for pertinent information—either instructions or text to be displayed—is called *parsing*. Any images, buttons, or icons that are referenced by URLs in the raw HTML document must be retrieved and loaded by the browser.

Different browsers will display the same Web page with slight style variances. For example, the elements of the page—headings, paragraphs, the block quote, emphasized text, and hypertext—are similar in function yet different in presentation depending on the browser. As you design your own Web pages, keep these presentation differences in mind. Try to make your pages attractive to all users, no matter which browser they choose.

There has been much ballyhoo about multimedia capabilities of the Web. Pictures, music, movies, sounds, and animation are among the media available to you. Yet media on the Internet is not broadcast the way television is; it must be downloaded to your computer and played like a laser disc or audio CD. To play or display media after it is retrieved from the Web, your browser enlists a group of computer programs known as *helper applications* (or simply "helper apps") to join its ranks. Your browser acts as manager of the smaller helper apps, calling them into action when you choose to view special media that it cannot display itself. When you select a media file—for instance, a short MPEG movie about the Amazon rain forest—your browser will automatically open the helper application that plays MPEG-format movies. (MPEG stands for Motion Picture Experts Group, and it is a common video format.) The helper application will then stay open until you choose to quit the program. For other media—like a WAV-format sound file—another helper application is opened.

Despite differences in their features, all browsers should parse a page, display images, and play multimedia in effectively the same way.

How Browsers Retrieve and Display Web Pages

When you want to view a Web page, your browser must do at least two jobs. First, it retrieves the text and any graphics for that page from another computer—a Web server. Next, the browser displays the data in a window on your computer screen.

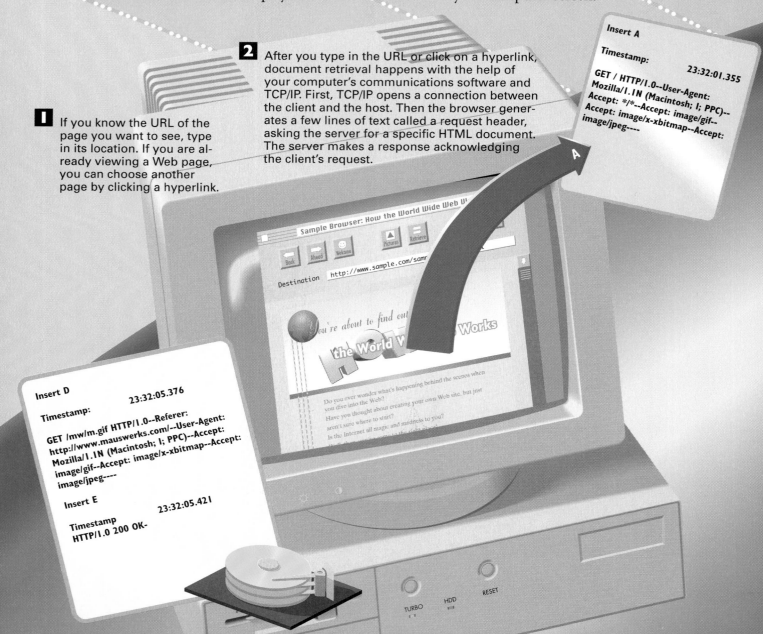

1 If you know the URL of the page you want to see, type in its location. If you are already viewing a Web page, you can choose another page by clicking a hyperlink.

2 After you type in the URL or click on a hyperlink, document retrieval happens with the help of your computer's communications software and TCP/IP. First, TCP/IP opens a connection between the client and the host. Then the browser generates a few lines of text called a request header, asking the server for a specific HTML document. The server makes a response acknowledging the client's request.

Insert A

Timestamp: 23:32:01.355

GET / HTTP/1.0--User-Agent: Mozilla/1.1N (Macintosh; I; PPC)-- Accept: */*--Accept: image/gif-- Accept: image/x-xbitmap--Accept: image/jpeg----

Insert D

Timestamp: 23:32:05.376

GET /mw/m.gif HTTP/1.0--Referer: http://www.mauswerks.com/--User-Agent: Mozilla/1.1N (Macintosh; I; PPC)--Accept: image/gif--Accept: image/x-xbitmap--Accept: image/jpeg----

Insert E

Timestamp 23:32:05.421

HTTP/1.0 200 OK-

3 The HTML document is sent as text from the server to the client through the TCP/IP pipeline. The client acknowledges receipt of the page and the connection is closed. The HTML document data is stored temporarily in your computer's memory or in a disk cache.

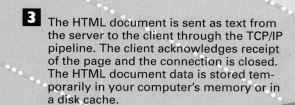

Insert B

Timestamp: 23:32:01.541

Server: Purveyor / v1.1 Windows NT--Allow: GET HEAD POST-- MIME-version: 1.0--Content-type: text/html--Date: Tuesday, 19-Sep -95 12:15:28 GMT--Last-modified: Wednesday, 1-Nov-95 00:34:04 GMT--Content-length: 598----

B

Insert   C

Timestamp   23:32:01.594

```
<HTML>
<HEAD>
<TITLE>
</HEAD>

<BODY>
<P> Do you ever wonder...

<P><IMG SRC = "Spider.GIF"

<HI> You'll learn about...

<A REF = "some URL"> Go to some URL</A>

<H2> Get ready to surf!

<P> As you cruise...
</BODY>
</HTML>
```

4 Parsing the HTML document happens next. Your browser scans each line of the newly received HTML document, beginning with the first line and working down. When a browser parses an HTML document it is looking for legitimate HTML tags—which usually format text or load images. Some browsers will display the text contained in the HTML document before images have loaded, so a user can beginning reading the page as soon as possible.

5 If the browser runs across HTML tags that link to images and pictures, then your browser will ask the server for the images. All further requests for images are made separately. So if five images appear within a Web page, a total of six separate requests are made of the server—one for the original HTML page and one for each of the five images.

Web Note

The computer code of any image can be expressed as text—albeit very confusing text. This way image files are sent within TCP/IP packets, just like HTML text documents. The most common image formats used for Web pages, GIF and JPEG, are called *run length encoded compressed* images. An image, displayed in its entirety, is positioned relative to text or other graphics as specified by the HTML tags.

CHAPTER
9

How Protocols Work

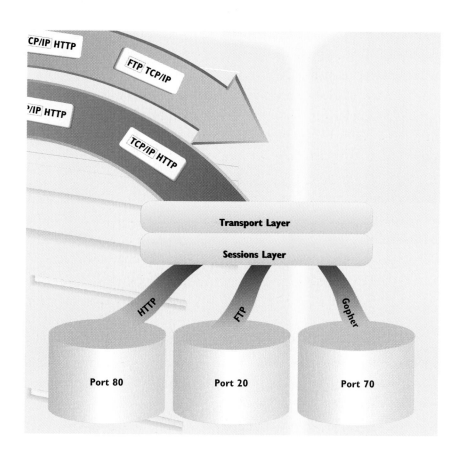

A protocol is a communications standard that many computers can understand. There are more protocols on the Internet than there are at a White House state dinner. Luckily, you can access most of the common protocols used on the Internet—such as HTTP, Gopher, FTP, WAIS, and NEWS—from your Web browser.

At the center of all Internet protocols is TCP/IP, or Transmission Control Protocol/Internet Protocol. This protocol suite is the base standard that enables transmission of data packets over the Internet. Other protocols that have more specific uses, such as transferring files between computers, sending mail, or quickly serving documents to clients, operate on top of TCP/IP. The following illustration shows packets of information being sent across the Internet. TCP/IP is like the cell wall of each packet and the HTTP, FTP, e-mail, or other information within that cell is much like the cell's nucleus. This model demonstrates how different protocols are similarly transmitted over the Internet using TCP/IP.

The oldest protocol used for transferring files from one computer to another via the Internet is the file transfer protocol, or FTP. Using FTP, you can retrieve, or "download," any file available on the Internet to your own computer. This protocol enables certain security measures that may restrict access to particular files and servers. However, if you do not have password right of entry, you may only be able to log onto a system anonymously with limited access. Once the file transfer is complete, you can use the file just as you would any other on your hard disk.

Gopher is a document transmission protocol. Unlike FTP, Gopher allows you to view documents online without having to download them to your PC's hard disk. Gopher menu items are all located together on one server, which means that unlike the Web it is a *nondistributed* system.

Of the hundreds of protocols on the Net, the World Wide Web uses only one: Hypertext Transfer Protocol, or HTTP. HTTP is a *stateless* protocol designed to transfer documents at a fast rate. Stateless systems do not remember any information from one document transfer to the next, or from one connection to another. If any other documents or files are needed, a new connection must be opened between computers, a new request and response made, and the connection closed. Also, the Web is a *distributed* system, which adds the ability to view and link to documents on any machine on the Internet.

Each of these protocols transfer computer files of all shapes and sizes. A Multipurpose Internet Mail Extension, or MIME, is a way for computers to keep track of multiple file types sent over the Internet. When your Web browser requests a Web page with a sound clip and two pictures, for example, there are four files with three different MIME *types* sent back: text, audio, and image. MIME types denote different media sent over computer networks; they are not protocols.

How a Protocol Works

Hundreds of protocols are used on the Internet. The World Wide Web is based on only one protocol: HTTP. However, many Web browsers can also access or display information transmitted by other protocols, such as FTP, Gopher, and e-mail. Each of these specialized protocols also use TCP/IP to route all of the data packets through the Internet.

In the OSI (open system interconnection) scheme, there are seven layers that are involved in implementing protocols.

	(The electronic signal sent over phone lines, etc.)
Physical Layer (connects nodes or connection points; passes bits)	
Data Link Layer (transmits data between nodes)	**Other Protocols**
Network Layer (routes data between stations)	
Transport Layer (facilitates end-to-end control)	**TCP/IP**
Session Layer (coordinates communications)	
Presentation Layer (syntax for conversion data)	**Web Browser**
Application Layer (reason for communicating)	

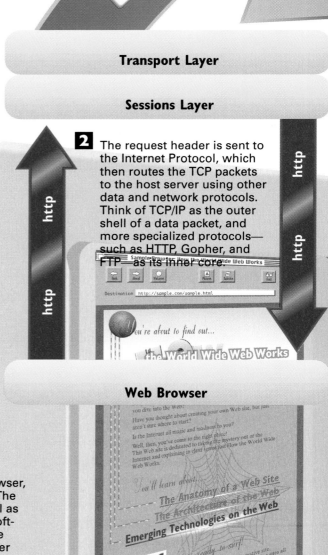

Transport Layer

Sessions Layer

2 The request header is sent to the Internet Protocol, which then routes the TCP packets to the host server using other data and network protocols. Think of TCP/IP as the outer shell of a data packet, and more specialized protocols—such as HTTP, Gopher, and FTP—as its inner core.

Web Browser

1 When you click on a hyperlink in your Web browser, a simple request for information is generated. The request contains the protocol to be used as well as the location of the linked document. The TCP software on your computer attaches a header to the data packet indicating the protocol, among other information (in this case, HTTP).

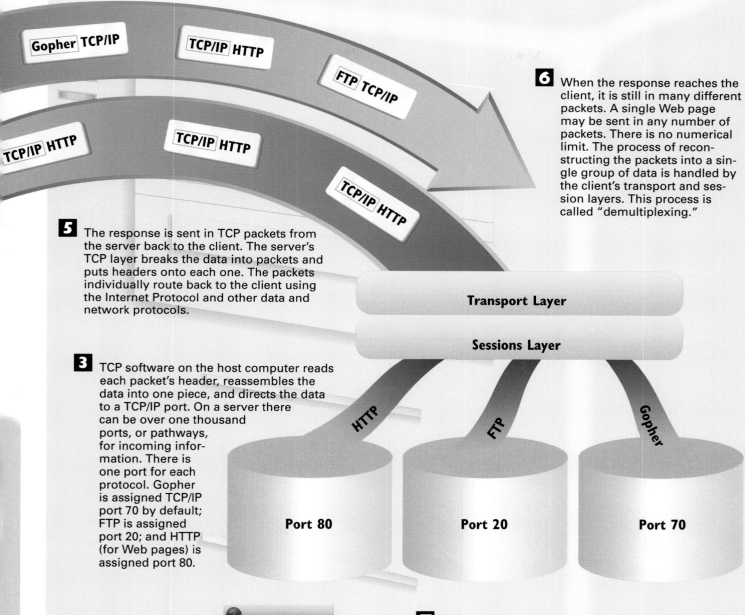

6 When the response reaches the client, it is still in many different packets. A single Web page may be sent in any number of packets. There is no numerical limit. The process of reconstructing the packets into a single group of data is handled by the client's transport and session layers. This process is called "demultiplexing."

5 The response is sent in TCP packets from the server back to the client. The server's TCP layer breaks the data into packets and puts headers onto each one. The packets individually route back to the client using the Internet Protocol and other data and network protocols.

Transport Layer

Sessions Layer

3 TCP software on the host computer reads each packet's header, reassembles the data into one piece, and directs the data to a TCP/IP port. On a server there can be over one thousand ports, or pathways, for incoming information. There is one port for each protocol. Gopher is assigned TCP/IP port 70 by default; FTP is assigned port 20; and HTTP (for Web pages) is assigned port 80.

HTTP

FTP

Gopher

Port 80

Port 20

Port 70

4 Server software specifically designed to handle a particular protocol then receives the data and executes any tasks at hand, such as document retrieval.

7 Your Web browser looks through the reassembled response data and determines what information it should display and what it should read for formatting or other instructions. (Recall that this process is called "parsing.") If any images or other media are required, the browser makes another request of the server and the process is repeated. (This is a drawback of "stateless" systems.) In ideal circumstances it should take only about 100ms (milliseconds) or so for the client to make a request and receive a response. In reality this kind of speed is rarely achieved for dial-up Internet users.

CHAPTER

10

CGI– The Common Gateway Interface

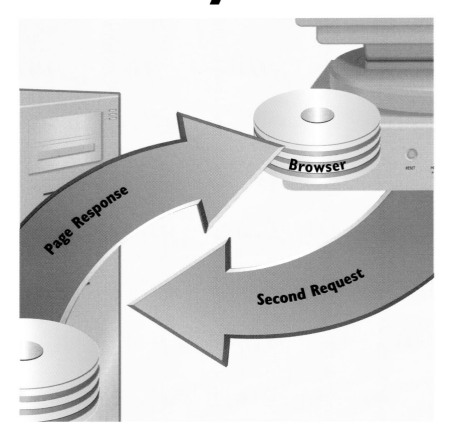

IF you browse the Web for very long you are sure to come across the term CGI, or *Common Gateway Interface.* CGI refers to the communications protocol by which a Web server can communicate with other applications. For example, a CGI application, sometimes called a "script," can transform a static image into a clickable image—called an *image map*—with various clickable parts. Both image maps and fill-out forms use CGI, which is an extension of the original capabilities of the Web and the HTTP protocol. However, the CGI is more sophisticated than the simpler HTTP protocol.

CGI and *CGI applications* are often confused. CGI applications receive data from the server and return the data via the Common Gateway Interface, or the CGI. The CGI is a standardized means of communication between a CGI application and the HTTP server. CGI applications are usually written in a programming language called Perl (Practical Extraction and Reporting Language), although they may be written in C, C++, Pascal, AppleScript, or others.

Both image maps and interactive forms require that customized data be sent from the client to the server, over to the CGI application for processing, and back again. Custom data is any unique information, such as the current date, your name and address, and even mouse click coordinates, which the Web server cannot handle without help. When customized data from an image map or an interactive form arrives at the server, it is redirected by the Web server to a CGI application through the CGI.

Image maps may be thought of as fancy hyperlinks. But instead of a word or entire icon or image linking to another page, an image is divided into coordinates, and different segments— or coordinates—link to different HTML pages. That is, image maps link to another document through a predefined "hot" area within an image. As soon as you click your mouse on a hot spot a CGI script and special image map coordinates file, with the suffix .map, go to work. A CGI application reads the map file to match coordinates of a mouse click with a corresponding URL. For instance, imagine an electronic map of the United States in which you click on Washington, D.C. In the HTML code for that page the electronic map is surrounded by a tag and an attribute called ISMAP. The code looks something like this:

```
<A HREF="some.server/maps/clickable.map>
<IMG SRC+"clickable.map" ISMAP>
</A>
```

The x and y coordinates of your mouse click are sent to the server because the ISMAP attribute is present. The coordinates are received by the server, and then redirected to a CGI application. The CGI application scans the file for matching coordinates, then forwards the corresponding

URL to the server. Lastly, if the Web page resides on the same server, it will deliver that Web page to the client browser. If not, the server returns the URL to the client browser, which in turn sends a request to the correct server for the page. You then see the page about Washington, D.C. begin to load on your browser. Behind the scenes, the server passed your mouse click coordinates to a CGI application via the CGI. Then the CGI application matched those coordinates to its URL in a .map file, then sent the URL back to the server, which redirected the client browser to the new Web page. Simple as that.

A three-part process begins when you provide information on a Web page designed to accept user input. First, you submit unique information—like a name or e-mail address—to the server for processing. Next, the server redirects the information to a CGI application that is called by the form *"submit."* CGI scripts are activated by the server in response to an HTTP request from the client. Lastly, a CGI application may send form data to another computer program, such as a database, save it to a file, or even generate a unique HTML document in response to the user's request. The technical name for this is an interactive form. Note that a CGI application is really a program, while the Common Gateway Interface is the "doorway" of sorts through which the Web server sends requests and the CGI application collects and returns data. In this example, a database can be the CGI application to which the Web server sends form data.

CGI scripts are invaluable yet invisible Web tools. Image maps make Web browsing more intuitive and fun. Interactive forms allow unique information to be constantly refreshed. The CGI helps transform the Web from a traditional text-based interface to an exciting interactive graphics interface.

URLS of Note

Image map examples: **http://www.777FILM.com/?TP:National+Lld:1** (map of the U.S.), **http://www.zdnet.com** (menu bar along top and left side of page)

Interactive form examples: **http://www.switchboard.com/** (an online phone book), **http://www.iplaza.com/colotrav/form.html** (Colorado travel guide feedback form)

How Image Maps and Interactive Forms Work

The Common Gateway Interface is a way to extend the capabilities of Web server software. CGI programs process unique information that cannot be processed by the Web server.

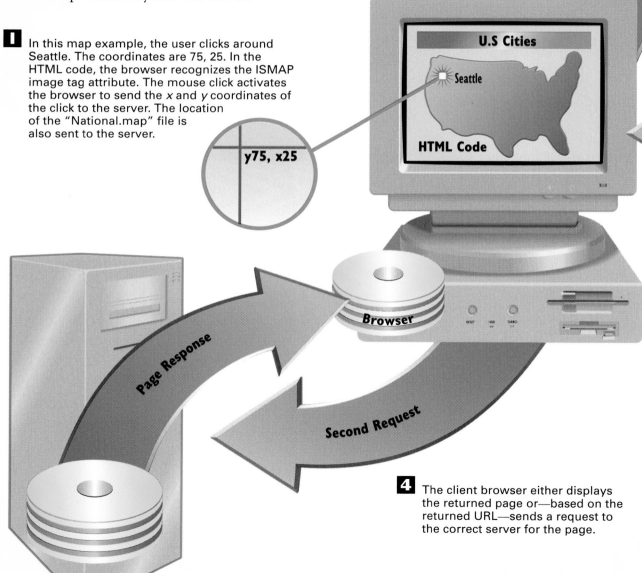

1 In this map example, the user clicks around Seattle. The coordinates are 75, 25. In the HTML code, the browser recognizes the ISMAP image tag attribute. The mouse click activates the browser to send the x and y coordinates of the click to the server. The location of the "National.map" file is also sent to the server.

y75, x25

U.S Cities

Seattle

HTML Code

Request

Page Response

Browser

RESET   HDD   TURBO

Second Request

4 The client browser either displays the returned page or—based on the returned URL—sends a request to the correct server for the page.

2 The server hands off the coordinate and map file data to a CGI application. The CGI application matches the coordinates to the correct URL. The URL is handed back to the server and the server sends the page to the client.

75, 25
samples. ISMAP

3 The Web document is either served up (if it resides on the same server) or the client browser is forwarded the new URL.

age or URL Response

Server
CGI App

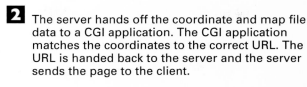

1 In working with an interactive form, the user clicks a data entry submit button. The data in the data fields is sent to the server with the request.

2 When a form submission is received by the server, it activates a CGI application. (The application could add the form data to a database or compare it to a password list of eligible users, among other tasks.) The program's output goes either to another program, like a database, or into a unique HTML document, or both.

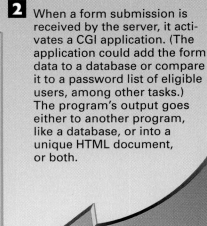

Sample Browser: How the World Wide Web Works

Destination sample.form

Name: John Doe

PERSONAL PREFERENCES

Color: Sky blue
Book: The Odyssey by Homer
City: Rio de Janeiro
Movie: Casablanca
Actor: Humphrey Bogart

Enter Data

Request

CGI App

CHAPTER

11

How the Host Server Works

IT'S not uncommon to hear the words "host" and "server" used interchangeably to mean the computer hardware that houses a Web site. For our purposes, though, we use "host" to refer to the hardware. In effect, this computer plays *host* to the Web site, managing the communications protocols and housing the pages and the related software required to create a Web site on the Internet. The host machine often uses the UNIX, Windows NT, or Macintosh operating systems, which have the TCP/IP protocols built in.

We use the term "server" to refer to the software that resides on the host and *serves up* the pages and otherwise acts on the requests sent from the client browser software. The server is not responsible for TCP/IP communications—the host operating system does that—instead, the server handles the HTTP requests and communications with the host operating system.

Your Web site host computer must have an Internet address. An *IP address,* a unique numbered name that looks something like 123.456.78.9, is necessary so that other computers on the Internet can locate and communicate with the host. Because people have a tough time remembering multidigit numbers, a host can also have a domain or server name that is, in essence, a nickname for the numeric IP address. When a host receives a request to connect to a domain name, it must first look up the corresponding IP address before it can actually find the host. The Domain Name Server, or DNS, is the system that does the matching of domain name to IP address. Without a DNS, you cannot get to the host unless you know its IP address.)

In order for a computer to act as a host, it must have either a leased line or dial-up connection to the Internet. If it uses the latter, the host must also have a SLIP or PPP account through an Internet service provider.

There are different types of server software (database servers or network servers, for example), performing different types of services for different types of clients. Specifically, a Web server is an HTTP server, and its function is to send information to the client software (typically a browser) using the Hypertext Transfer Protocol. (For more on HTTP, see Chapter 9.)

Usually, the client browser requests that the server return an HTML document. Technically, that exchange looks something like this:

```
GET /docs/index.html HTTP/1.0
Accept: text/plain
Accept: applications/x-html
Accept: applications/html
Accept: text/html
```

These lines are sent from the client and, in essence, are saying: "Send the file index.html found in the directory /docs/ using the HTTP protocol, so long as the file is either plain text or HTML." The GET header tells the server what the client wants and the Accept headers tell the server what formats the client can receive. Accept headers are MIME types, a series of defined data types that enable the client and server to handle the data they send back and forth. (MIME is explained more fully in Chapter 9.)

The server receives this request and sends back a response. The top portion of the response includes transmission information, and the rest of the response is the HTML file. A typical response looks something like this:

Transmission Information

```
HTTP /1.0 200 OK
Date: Monday, 01-Jan-96 12:01:00
Server: NCSA/1.3
MIME-version 1.0
Content-type: text/html
```

HTML File

```
<html>
<head>
<title> Welcome to our Web page </title>
</head>
<body>
<H1> Welcome to our Web page </H1>
<p> Thanks for dropping by the <em> How the World Wide Web Works
</em> page.

<p> This page is an evolving example of the things you're reading
about in the illustrated book <em> How the World Wide Web Works
</em>. Be sure to come by often to learn more about the exciting
changes happening on the Web.
</body>
</html>
```

The server is saying to the browser, "Here are a few things you need to know about the server you've just contacted, along with the page you requested, sent as an HTML file in plain text." The Content-type header tells the browser it is sending the MIME type text/html, which confirms that the document is an HTML page.

A Web server does more than send pages to the browser, however. It passes requests to run common gateway interface (CGI) scripts to the CGI applications. These scripts run external mini-programs, such as a database lookup. The server sends the script to the application via the CGI and communicates the results of the script back to the browser, if appropriate. (For more on CGI, see Chapter 10.) Moreover, the server software includes configuration files and utilities to secure and manage the Web site in a variety of ways.

How the Web Server Software Works

Client (browser) software sends its request for data to the host, where the request is processed by the Web server software.

Request from Browser

Included in the browser's request is the information wanted and the file formats the browser can accept.

If the browser asks for an HTML file, the Web server retrieves the file, attaches a header to the file, and sends it to the browser.

Returns HTML page to Client

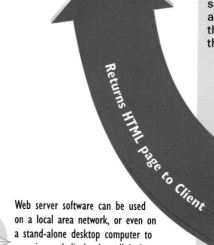

Web Server

EXE.

LOGS

Server Root

Welcome Page

HTML documents

Document Root

IP address
83.382.1.838

Web server software can be used on a local area network, or even on a stand-alone desktop computer to organize and display hyperlinked documents—without ever connecting to the Internet.

If the browser has asked for specific database information, the Web server will pass a request through the CGI to the application, which performs a database lookup, for example. The CGI script returns the results to the Web server, which in turn attaches a header to the data and sends it to the browser.

Because a computer with a single IP address can host several types of servers, the address may need to include a port number to identify the correct server, if it is one other than the IP's default server. Each port is associated with a particular server. Ports are identified by a number from 0 to 65,535, but common server types, such as FTP servers, by convention are given the same number.

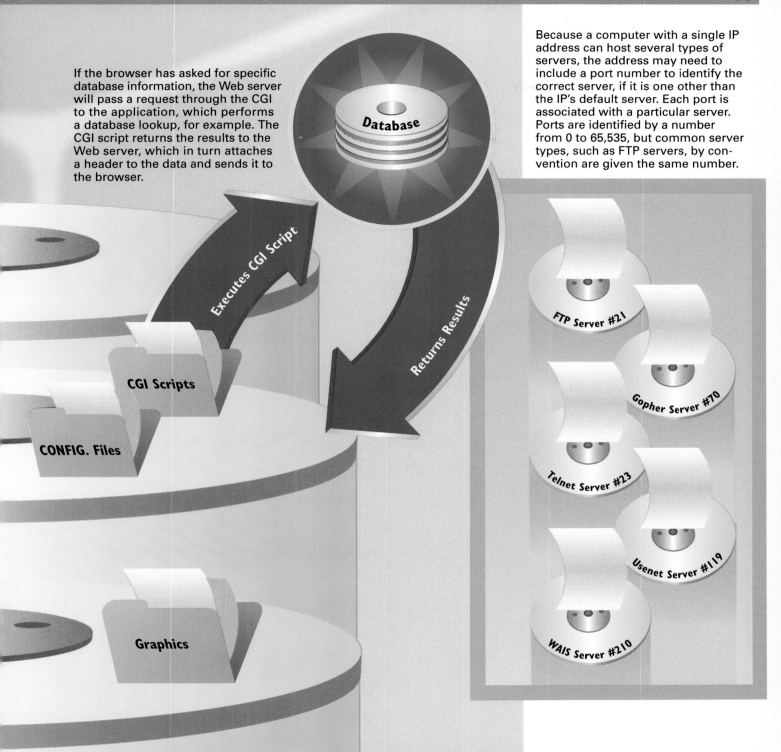

Database

Executes CGI Script

Returns Results

CGI Scripts

CONFIG. Files

Graphics

FTP Server #21

Gopher Server #70

Telnet Server #23

Usenet Server #119

WAIS Server #210

Domain name

books.zdp.com

The host computer must have a unique IP address in order to send and receive information across the Internet. Because raw IP addresses are very intimidating, they are assigned a unique domain name, which is less daunting. The domain name is part of a hierarchical lookup system called the Domain Name System (DNS).

CHAPTER

12

Communications on the Web

WE'VE talked about the browser software on the client end of an Internet connection, and the Web server software on the host end. But what's the "magic in the middle" that lets the two sides talk to one another? The heart of communications across the Internet is a set of protocols called TCP/IP, or Transmission Control Protocol/Internet Protocol. These related protocols set forth the rules by which computers exchange messages and share resources across a computer network. No matter who makes the computer, how it is designed, or what operating system it runs, computers running operating systems and communications software that adhere to the TCP/IP protocol suite can communicate with one another.

In simplest terms, data sent across the Internet is broken into pieces and put in packages using this protocol. The packages travel across the Internet—sometimes following different routes—and are reassembled when they arrive at their destination. (For more details on the TCP/IP protocols, see Chapter 9.)

The TCP/IP protocol is part of the transport layer of the communications software or the operating system of both the client and host. The UNIX operating system used by many host machines has TCP/IP built in. Windows-based computers use Windows sockets, or WinSock, and Macintosh computers use Mac TCP application interface as the communications layer between the browser and the operating system.

Of course, the core of the package is the data. But without the TCP/IP protocols, the bundle wouldn't travel very far—in fact, it wouldn't travel at all. TCP, or Transmission Control Protocol, is the part of the package that contains the information about taking apart the data and putting it back together in the right order. Before sending the data, TCP breaks it into pieces and attaches to each piece information about where that piece fits in the larger data chain. This information is essential, because data packets may travel different routes or may be delayed as they are sent across the network. TCP tells the computer at the receiving end how to reassemble the pieces in the proper order.

TCP is a connection-oriented protocol, meaning that communications between the client and host must be established via a handshake and maintained throughout the transmission. The *handshake* is a verification that the sending and receiving systems are "speaking the same language" and are using the same protocols to exchange data. The high-pitched squeal you hear when your modem connects with another is the way modems indicate a handshake. While the two computers are connected, TCP verifies that all data is transmitted—and retransmitted, if necessary—until it arrives at its destination correctly.

The IP, or Internet Protocol, contains the addressing information used as the data travels across the network to route the package to its proper destination. Each computer on the Internet has a unique *IP address*. The IP address is a numeric address that uniquely identifies a host computer on the Internet. Because people more easily remember names than they do numbers, these IP addresses are most often "nicknamed" with an easier-to-remember *host* or *domain name,* such as www.zdpress.com, that is the unique name of the host computer. As data packets travel the Internet, the IP protocol looks at routing tables that contain the addresses of host computers to find the route that will get the package to the correct host computer. These tables reside on computers throughout the Internet called, appropriately enough, routers. Domain Name Servers (DNS) are computers that match the computer's "nickname" with its proper IP address.

Occasionally, you may enter a URL into your browser, and after the brower has sent the request, you will receive a message back saying that the address cannot be found. The message typically reads something like "The domain cannot be located." In these instances, the domain name in the URL does not match any domain name listed on the DNS, and therefore cannot be matched to an IP address and be properly routed—sort of like sending a letter to an address where there is no house or building. Often, in these cases, you've mistyped the URL, and a quick correction will fix the problem.

Once the individual data packets reach a host, the TCP protocol at the host computer is used to put the data from the packets back together in its proper sequence.

Every computer connecting to the Internet must have a unique IP address in order to send and receive data packets. Individuals with dial-up access to the Internet rely on a temporary IP address assigned by their Internet service provider when the individual logs on. Internet service providers are companies that have made a business out of providing Internet connections to individuals who can't link directly to the Internet. These companies have host computers with many access ports that feed into the Internet backbone. When you connect to the Internet via an access provider, you are given a temporary, or dynamic, IP address, used to identify your computer while you are connected to the access provider's host.

In order to make a connection to the service provider and receive a temporary IP address, however, you need to use communications software that offers either a SLIP (Serial Line Internet Protocol) or PPP (Point to Point Protocol) connection. These two protocols handle data transfer and error checking necessary to send data over phone lines.

TCP and IP protocols are used together to handle many types of data transfer protocols, including HTTP, FTP, Telnet, and SMTP (Simple Mail Transport Protocol), among others. But because the functions of packaging the data and addressing it are separate, the IP protocol can be used with the User Datagram Protocol (UDP), a connectionless protocol, in applications where the error correction is not necessary.

These days, most users never even see these protocols. Most Internet or Web browser software programs make the communications layer transparent to the user: Simply install the browser software bundle and the communications protocol dirty work is done for you. Then, with these pieces in place, you're ready to make your Web connection.

Communicating across the Internet

To most consumers, the communications portion of the Web connection is invisible. The communications software and protocol settings are handled by the installation routine of the commercial Web browser. As a result, users interact with the Web through the browser, and they rarely ever see what's happening behind the scenes.

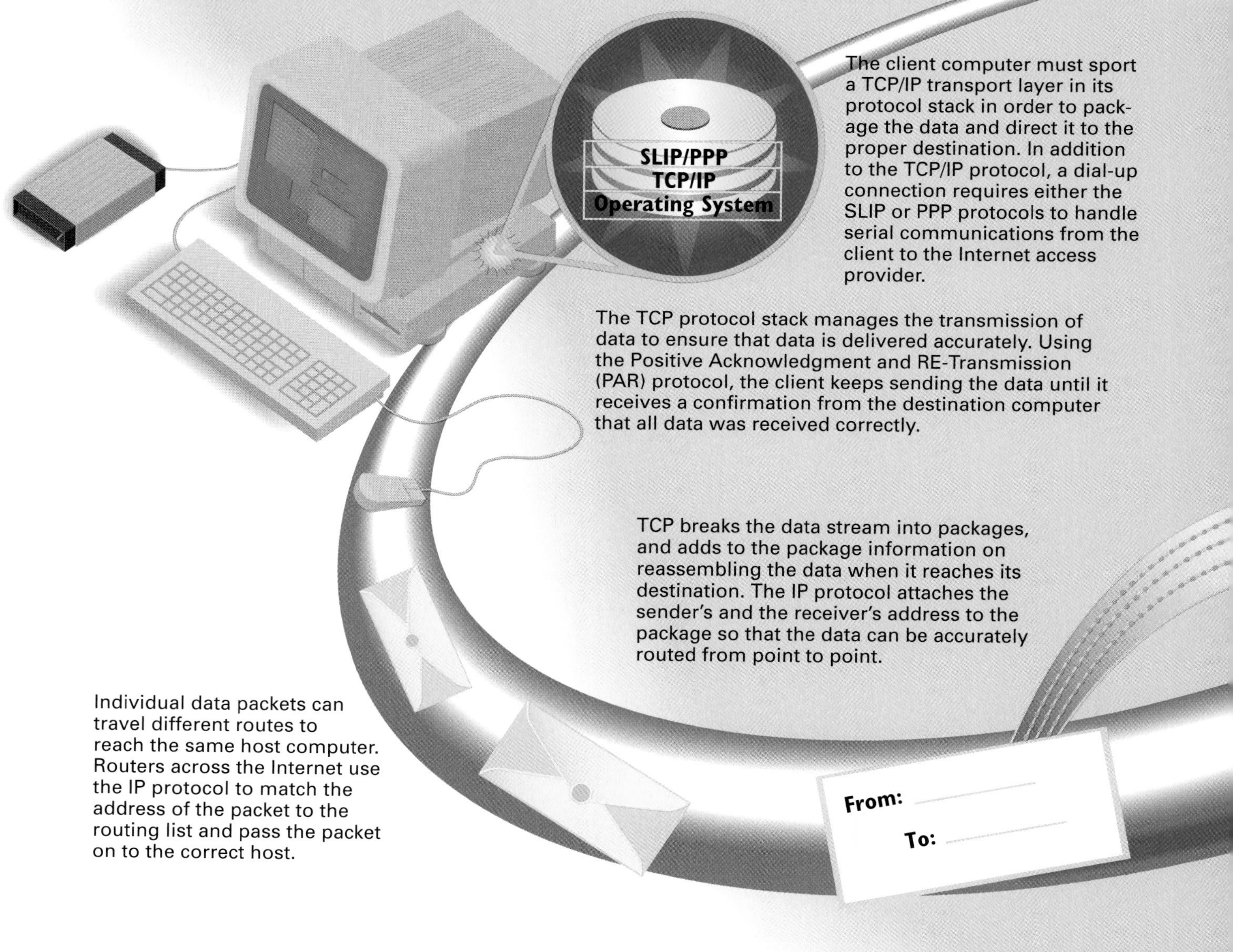

Backbone

SLIP/PPP
TCP/IP
Operating System

The client computer must sport a TCP/IP transport layer in its protocol stack in order to package the data and direct it to the proper destination. In addition to the TCP/IP protocol, a dial-up connection requires either the SLIP or PPP protocols to handle serial communications from the client to the Internet access provider.

The TCP protocol stack manages the transmission of data to ensure that data is delivered accurately. Using the Positive Acknowledgment and RE-Transmission (PAR) protocol, the client keeps sending the data until it receives a confirmation from the destination computer that all data was received correctly.

TCP breaks the data stream into packages, and adds to the package information on reassembling the data when it reaches its destination. The IP protocol attaches the sender's and the receiver's address to the package so that the data can be accurately routed from point to point.

Individual data packets can travel different routes to reach the same host computer. Routers across the Internet use the IP protocol to match the address of the packet to the routing list and pass the packet on to the correct host.

From: _____
To: _____

Users dialing into the Internet via modem must go through an ISP (Internet service provider) in order to connect to the Internet backbone. The access provider has multiple connections to simultaneously support many dial-in users. When you dial into an access provider's host computer, your connection is issued a temporary, or dynamic, IP address so that data returning from the destination host computer can be routed properly back to your computer.

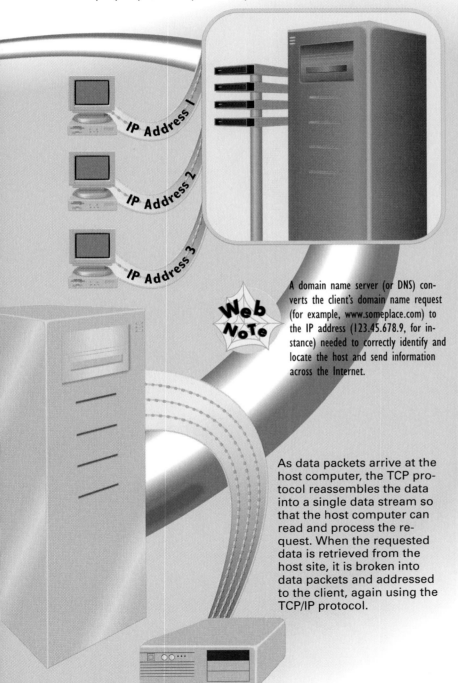

A domain name server (or DNS) converts the client's domain name request (for example, www.someplace.com) to the IP address (123.45.678.9, for instance) needed to correctly identify and locate the host and send information across the Internet.

As data packets arrive at the host computer, the TCP protocol reassembles the data into a single data stream so that the host computer can read and process the request. When the requested data is retrieved from the host site, it is broken into data packets and addressed to the client, again using the TCP/IP protocol.

Data Moves at Different Speeds

Many Web pages contain thousands of bytes of text and graphics material that must be transferred from a host computer to your client PC. The faster your Internet connection, the more information is transferred at one time and the faster it is displayed in the client browser—and the more enjoyable the Web surfing is.

Time to Transfer 1 Megabyte of Information across the Web

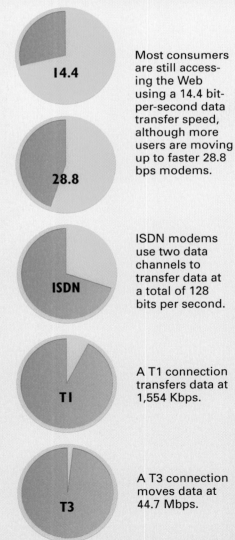

Most consumers are still accessing the Web using a 14.4 bit-per-second data transfer speed, although more users are moving up to faster 28.8 bps modems.

ISDN modems use two data channels to transfer data at a total of 128 bits per second.

A T1 connection transfers data at 1,554 Kbps.

A T3 connection moves data at 44.7 Mbps.

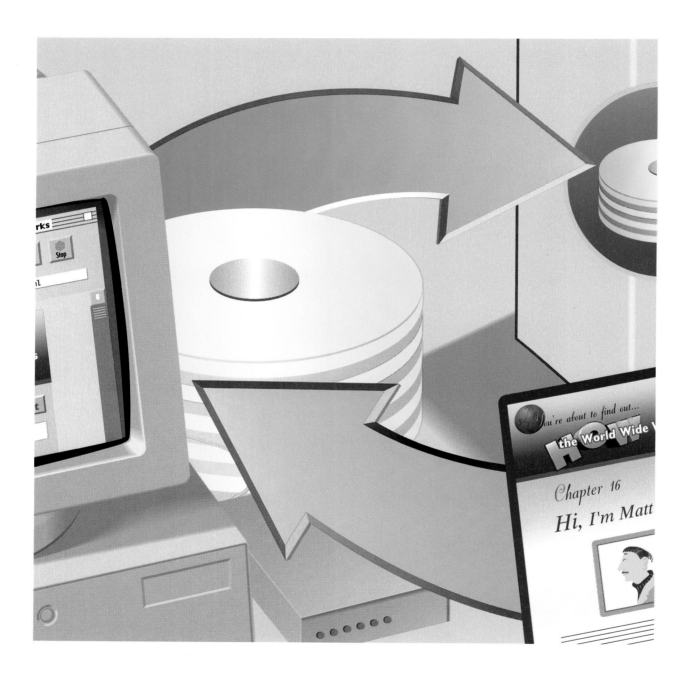

P A R T

MULTIMEDIA ON THE WEB

As the World Wide Web expands, bright and inventive minds are creating new ways to enhance the Web as a new communication medium. If formatted text and colorful graphics are good, imagine what animation, sound, and video can do to enhance communication. Why not use the Web to facilitate discussion, both in text and with voice? Or as a "front-end" to access all that data socked away in private and public data banks. Imagine three-dimensional graphics used to create "virtual" worlds that you can move around in and explore. As more ideas come to the fore, new multimedia and database searching technologies are being developed to support them.

Streaming audio enables sound files to be transmitted across the Internet and played on the client PC as the data streams in; no waiting to download large sound files before you can play them back. There are several technologies that make this possible, the most widely used of which is known as RealAudio. In its newest version, RealAudio 2.0 enables live audio broadcasts across the Web. In fact, President Clinton's 1996 State of the Union address was broadcast live over the Web using this technology, and a number of innovative people are creating Internet "radio stations."

If still images can communicate information adequately, imagine the powerful way ideas could be relayed if those images were able to move. Animation technologies such as server push and Shockwave do just that—they make it relatively easy for Web page developers to include moving graphics in their sites. And like streaming audio, the animation technologies are optimized for speedy transfer across Internet lines.

Java, a compact and portable programming language, is also being put to work on the Web. Because Java code can be executed on computers regardless of their operating system, programmers can write tiny applications that will run inside a Web browser whether that browser is running on a Windows, Mac, or UNIX operating system. The introduction of Java to the Web has sparked creative and very useful sites. A bank, for example, might create a Web site that includes information about their loan products. A loan calculator written in Java would let the customer calculate mortgage payments. With the result in hand, the customer could then apply for a loan from the bank—all by visiting a single site.

These animation and voice annotation technologies are creating dynamic Web sites that make it easier for Web surfers to get at more and better information. In fact, many of these tools are being linked to corporate and public databases, letting users conduct their own searches for information. One striking example is the Federal Express package tracking system. By connecting to the FedEx Web site (http://www.fedex.com/), you can search the company's package tracking database and find out for yourself if your overnight letter has reached its destination. This service has helped FedEx customers and enabled FedEx to cut down significantly on customer support calls.

It only stands to reason that a communications medium based on the world's telecommunications infrastructure would facilitate discussions, and the Web certainly does that. Internet Relay Chat, for example, enables people around the world to connect to a site and conduct text-based discussions. Rather hear someone's voice? A number of developers are working on systems that will transmit voices over the Internet, using the Web as the interface. There's even an effort underway called CU-SeeMe that provides video conferencing capabilities to properly equipped Web users.

Virtual reality is becoming a reality on the Web, too. Virtual Reality Modeling Language, or VRML, takes images into the third dimension. Using VRML—and many new development tools to facilitate VRML coding—Web publishers can create 3-D worlds that users can navigate freely. With a VRML-enabled browser, you retrieve a VRML page and then "look around" the 3-D space by moving your mouse cursor around the screen.

These are just a few—and the most well-progressed—of the multimedia technologies that are arriving on the Web scene. We will take a look at each of these more closely in the following chapters.

CHAPTER

13 Streaming Audio on the Web

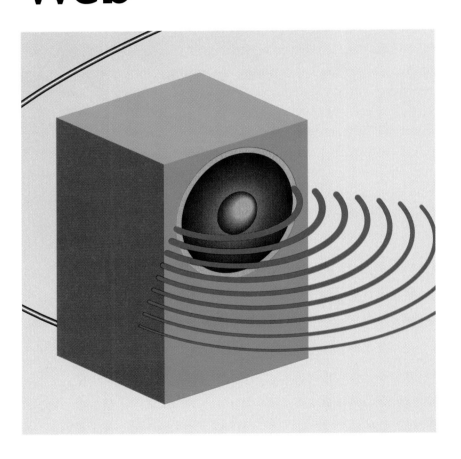

IT'S not enough anymore to surf the Web to see what's there; these days you can tune your browser to the Web to *hear* what's going on. Several advances in streaming audio technology make it possible to listen to spoken words, music—virtually any recording—even as the sound file is delivered to your computer. *Streaming* audio differs from downloadable audio files in that you can begin to hear and work with the file (fast forwarding or rewinding the audio) even before it has been completely downloaded to your computer. Once the audio file has made its way to your computer you can decide whether you want to save it to your hard drive or discard it.

The most widely adopted practical streaming or *real-time* audio technology for the Web is RealAudio, developed by Progressive Networks in Seattle, although several other firms are working on similar technology now. RealAudio was a breakthrough because it allowed streaming audio to be delivered across standard 14.4 bps modems. Earlier techniques, such as MBone, delivered streaming audio but required high-speed T1 lines to deliver good quality sound. Other companies, including StreamWorks (Xing) and VocalTec (Internet Wave) are also working on streaming audio and video. This chapter will focus on how streaming audio works, using RealAudio as the primary example and recognizing that other streaming audio technologies work similarly.

Before Progressive Networks brought its RealAudio technology to the Web, you had to download a proprietary digital sound file (a .AU, .SND, or .WAV file typically) to your local computer, and then open a separate audio player application to listen to it. Using streaming audio, you listen to the audio file as it is being sent to your system. In essence, the audio data streams across the Internet in a fashion analogous to the way a radio broadcast streams across the airwaves, playing as the sound reaches the radio, for example. But unlike radio, the audio file is cached in RAM on the client computer, so that you can rewind and replay the piece. It is only saved to the client's hard disk if you choose to do so. This streaming technology eliminates the waiting time to download a file, and enables Web site developers to seamlessly incorporate sound into their Web pages in a sensory experience that makes the site seem alive and active.

In order to incorporate streaming audio into a Web site, the Webmaster—the person who builds and maintains a site—must either have pre-recorded audio files or equipment to record digital sound, and must have the encoder and server software necessary to process audio files and serve streaming audio to the client. Let's use RealAudio as an example.

The Webmaster needs to have the RealAudio server software deliver sound in much the same way the Web server software delivers HTML pages. At the local computer, users need a RealAudio player—or plug-in—for their Netscape-compatible browser. (For more on browser helper or plug-in applications, see Chapter 8.) The RealAudio server and the plug-in app work in conjunction with the Web server and client browser, respectively.

RealAudio sound files are converted from the computer's native sound format to streaming audio format using the RealAudio encoder. For example, to create a RealAudio file, you record a sound just like you would capture any other audio for a computer: the audio source is fed into a sound card, and the sound is captured into a digital audio file format such as a .AU or .WAV file. Once the digital audio file is saved, it or any other audio file can be processed through the RealAudio encoder and published as a .RA (RealAudio) file to the RealAudio server. Everything you need to create a RealAudio file and sample the server is available at the Progressive Networks Web site at http://www.realaudio.com/. Progressive Networks charges Web site developers to use the encoder and server; individuals can download and use the RealAudio plug-in or player at no cost.

RealAudio 2.0 also offers a feature that enables Web site developers to embed URLs into the audio stream feed from the server to the local player. In this way, the developer can synchronize words and music with graphics or entire Web pages to create a self-running movie of sorts. When the RealAudio player encounters URLs, it sends them to the browser, which then launches requests to the appropriate Web server.

RealAudio has garnered some 3 million users and is quickly becoming the most commonly used tool for streaming audio on the Web. Moreover, Progressive Networks led the way for other "time-based" media, such as animation and motion video, enabling moving images to be delivered in real time over the Internet. For example, a company called Gold Disk is developing the Astound Web Player that streams multimedia files across the Web in much the same fashion that RealAudio streams sound files. And even Progressive Networks says it's "polishing its protocols" to deliver "time-based media" in applications created with other development tools such as Macromedia's Shockwave and Sun Microsystem's Java.

All of these developments point to a World Wide Web that is much more graphically and audibly exciting than the text and still images that have been most common on Web pages up until now.

URLs of Note

RealAudio: **http://www.realaudio.com/**

Wine Valley Radio (a RealAudio Internet radio station): **http://www.bpe.com/**

Radio.net: **http://www.netradio.net/**

Radio Internet: **http://www.fred.net/malta/radio.html**

The MBONE FAQ: **http://www.best.com/~prince/techinfo/mbone.faq.html/**

ToolVox for the Web: **http://www.voxware.com/tvweb.htm/**

Media Cast: **http://www.mediacast.com/MediaCast/instructions.html/**

How RealAudio Works

RealAudio uses digital technology that enables you to hear audio as it is delivered from the host computer to your local PC. Before you can hear streaming RealAudio files on your local computer, you must download the RealAudio Player plug-in for your Netscape browser. You can find the Player at http://www.realaudio.com/.

HTML Page Request

http://www.playlist.com/index.html

Streaming Audio R...

http://...nextpic.htr

Web Browser
Real Audio Player
Helper App

Real Audio Request

1 Links to RealAudio sounds are embedded into an HTML page much like any other hyperlink, but when you click on the link, the Netscape compatible browser passes the request for the RealAudio file off to the RealAudio Player helper app rather than sending the request to the host server.

2 The RealAudio Player then contacts a host computer where the RealAudio Server resides. The RealAudio Server receives the request for an audio stream, which is then sent from the server to the player. As the audio stream reaches the local computer, the player plays the audio through the computer's speakers.

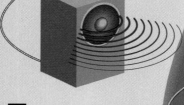

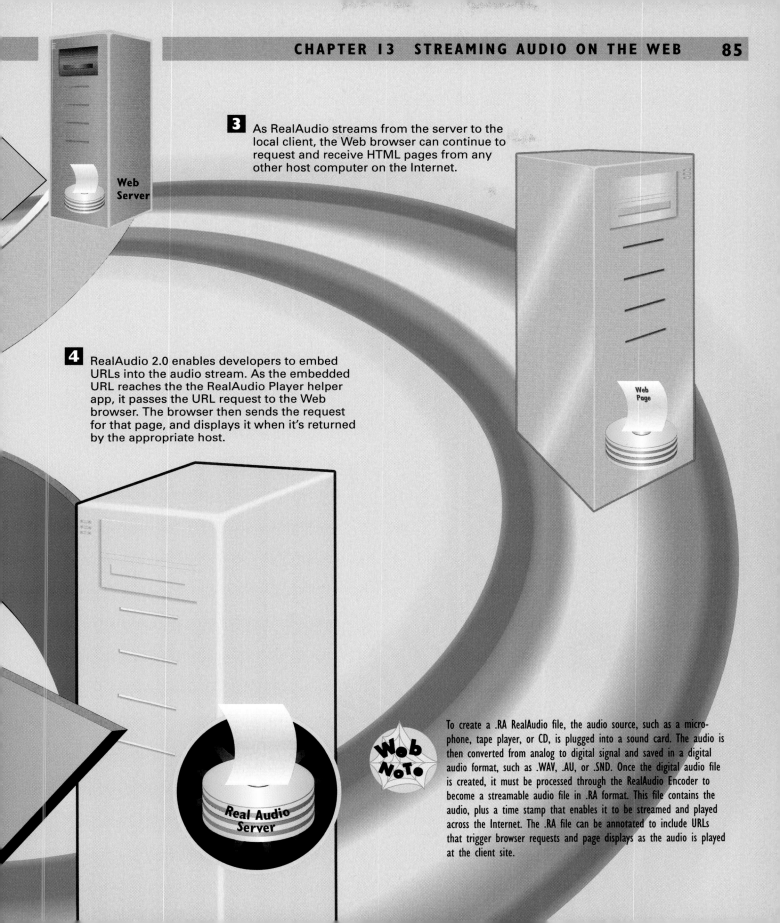

3 As RealAudio streams from the server to the local client, the Web browser can continue to request and receive HTML pages from any other host computer on the Internet.

4 RealAudio 2.0 enables developers to embed URLs into the audio stream. As the embedded URL reaches the the RealAudio Player helper app, it passes the URL request to the Web browser. The browser then sends the request for that page, and displays it when it's returned by the appropriate host.

Web Server

Web Page

Real Audio Server

Web NoTo

To create a .RA RealAudio file, the audio source, such as a microphone, tape player, or CD, is plugged into a sound card. The audio is then converted from analog to digital signal and saved in a digital audio format, such as .WAV, .AU, or .SND. Once the digital audio file is created, it must be processed through the RealAudio Encoder to become a streamable audio file in .RA format. This file contains the audio, plus a time stamp that enables it to be streamed and played across the Internet. The .RA file can be annotated to include URLs that trigger browser requests and page displays as the audio is played at the client site.

C H A P T E R

14

Animation on the Web

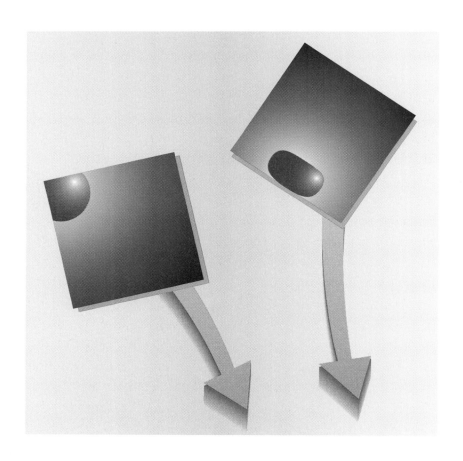

IMAGINE drawing a tiny animated figure in the margins of this book. The figure you draw might bend down, pick up a ball, and throw it across the page. You would have a simple example of how all animation works. Just like in a flip-book, animation on the Web is a series of still images displayed in succession to create an illusion of fluid motion. The faster the frames advance, the more fluid the animation becomes. Unfortunately, the Web can be a very slow place, and an animation that should run quickly often crawls across the screen.

The Netscape Navigator Web browser is quickly becoming a very popular browser because it supports many media types. For example, Netscape's Navigator software supports the ability for a server to *push* and a client to *pull* an animation and a relatively newer concept known as *animated GIFS*. *Client pull* happens when an HTML page gives instructions to the browser to request and load another document automatically. This feature is like a slide show. Web pages are displayed one after the other with a specified time delay in between. This is useful for step-by-step instructions or movie-like credits, for example. Yet client pull is slowed by the need to load a whole page rather than a single cell of animation, which prevents the illusion of fluid animation. The frames feature of Netscape 2.0 has given new life to client pull. Rather than the whole window changing, only an isolated frame reloads automatically.

Client pull requests are embedded within the HTTP response header of a Web page sent back from the server to the client. The META tag inserts *meta-information* into a response header. Meta-information is used to help parse a Web page but it is not displayed by the browser. A response header is literally the beginning of each HTTP response that a server sends back to a client with the requested Web page.

The line of meta-information used for client pull consists of a *refresh* command, followed by a number and an optional URL. The number indicates the number of seconds before the same page automatically reloads itself. If the URL is present, the browser waits a specified number of seconds, then sends a request for the document referenced by the URL.

Server push is a complement to client pull, though server push is the more complex of the two. The difference is that server push requires a CGI (Common Gateway Interface) script that tells the server when to automatically serve a new document or image. It requires the client browser to be able to recognize the MIME-type called *multipart/x-mixed-replace*. This MIME-type allows for multiple documents to be sent within one message. To understand how server push works, imagine an e-mail message with text, hypertext, a digital movie and sound, and you can see how multiple "documents" (media types) can be sent within a single message. The multipart message is simply a series of images that display one right after the other, each being sent or "pushed" by the server. In this way a small animation can be nicely embedded among the text and images of an otherwise static Web page.

To make a server push animation, a series of images must be created. Just like flip-book animation, these images are designed to show fluid motion. Usually these are saved as *GIF* images. GIF stands for *Graphics Interchange Format* and is the most popular format for all of the image files seen on the Web.

Second, a CGI script must be either created from scratch or reused with the programmer's permission. This script uses the multipart/x-mixed-replace MIME-type to arrange the series of GIF images in order. As the animation runs, the first image will be replaced by the second image, which will be replaced by the third image, and so on.

The HTML page with an inline animation (that is, an animation that you can see right on the page, without any external helper applications running) references that animation with the standard image tag <IMG>, the HTML command for "put this image here." But instead of calling a static GIF image, the URL references the CGI script. As the CGI script displays one GIF image after the other, a simple animation is created.

Animated GIFs are a series of graphical GIF images that "roll up" into a single image—much like the flip book "animates" a series of drawings as you thumb through the pages. These animated GIFs load into a browser just like any other GIF file, but do so in a series to give the illusion of motion. Animated GIFs have the added benefit of speed because images are cached in memory on the client PC and loaded from memory rather than from across the Internet. They work with any browser, too, because if the browser can't recognize the GIFs as a series, it loads only the first frame. Best of all, they don't require scripting, and so they represent an easy solution to adding motion to Web pages.

Recently more complex multimedia animation has become possible using Sun Microsystems's Java language and Macromedia's Shockwave plug-in for Netscape. (Currently only the Netscape Navigator 2.0 browser supports the Shockwave plug-in.) We can expect to see competing products from other companies, but for now Shockwave has established itself as the leader in multimedia on the Web.

Shockwave plays multimedia, complete with sounds and interactivity, that was created with Macromedia's popular Director and Authorware programs. An animation created and viewed with Shockwave requires three general steps. First, the animation must be created with either Director or Authorware. Second, the animation, or "movie," must be converted to the Shockwave file format with another application from Macromedia called Afterburner. Third, the Shockwave plug-in for Netscape Navigator 2.0 plays the Shockwave animation on the Web within the browser window. Like all helper applications and plug-ins, you must first download and install the Shockwave plug-in before you can view any "shocked" Web pages.

URLs of Note

Client pull animation: **http://speakeasy.org/~south/** (click on the "Welcome" frame)

Server push animation: **http://heasarc.gsfc.nasa.gov/** (all three in-line an animation), **http://www.levi.com/menu, http://speakeasy.org/~south/where.html**

Shockwave animation: **http://www.macromedia.com/Tools/Shockwave/Gallery/Vanguard**

How Animation on the Web Works

Two popular animation methods on the Web are *client pull* and *server push*. Currently, only Netscape Navigator browsers support these.

Client Pull

Client pull is executed by the "refresh" command. A refresh command is written into an HTML document using the META tag. The contents of the META tag are added to the header's meta-information sent from the server along with the HTTP response. During a client pull sequence the browser reads this header information, which instructs it to keep track of the time elapsed between pages retrieved with the help of your PC's internal clock. When the time has elapsed, the browser requests and displays the next page.

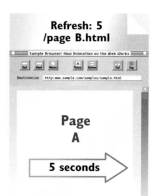
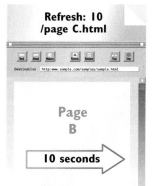
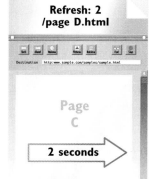

Refresh: 5 /page B.html — Page A — 5 seconds

Refresh: 10 /page C.html — Page B — 10 seconds

Refresh: 2 /page D.html — Page C — 2 seconds

Refresh: 5 http://www.server.com/folder/page E.html — Page D — 5 seconds

Refresh: /page F.ht — Page F

1 The "refresh" command does two things: First, it indicates the time before the next page request is sent or the same page reloads. For example, page A in the illustration will refresh after 5 seconds. Secondly, if the URL follows the number of seconds, a request for that page will be sent automatically after 5 seconds. After the browser parses a document's meta-information and recognizes the "refresh" command in the header, it knows to send a request for the page indicated by the URL following the command.

2 If the next document to load also has a "refresh" command in the header, then the browser will simply repeat the process. In this case it will retrieve and display page C after 10 seconds.

3 Whoever writes the HTML source code can specify how long it will be until the request for the next page is made. Page C will refresh after only 2 seconds, followed by page D.

4 Each page in a client pull sequence can be located anywhere on the Web. The URL following the "refresh" command may lead the browser to any active server. Page E is located on a different server than pages A–D but will still be requested automatically after 5 seconds.

A client pull sequence may continue for as many or as few pages as the site designer wants. The last page will simply not have a "refresh" command in the header. A user may stop the process manually by clicking the browser's Stop button.

Server Push

Server push is more complicated than client pull, but it allows for inline animation that does not require an entire Web page to load each animation frame.

1 The HTML source code for a server push animation is deceptively simple. The animation is referenced by the <IMG> (image) tag just like a static picture or icon.

html page

<HI>Page Heading CHI></HI>
<IMG SRC="http://some.server/
animation.cgi>
<P>
Body text text text text text
text text...

2 When the browser recognizes the <IMG> tag it makes a single request to the server for a file. But rather than retrieving an image file, the HTML reference tag <IMG SCR="URL"> gives directions to a CGI script that runs the animation.

Internet

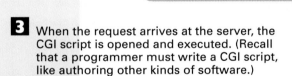

How Animation
on the Web Works

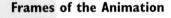

3 When the request arrives at the server, the CGI script is opened and executed. (Recall that a programmer must write a CGI script, like authoring other kinds of software.)

CGI Script

multipart/x-replace

: frame 1

-Boundary-

file: frame 2

-Boundary-

file: frame 3

-Boundary-

file: frame 4 etc.

Frames of the Animation

4 The CGI script takes advantage of the *multipart/x-mixed-replace* MIME type. This allows the CGI script to send, or "push," a series of still images from the server to the client as if it were transferring a single file. In this illustration the animation has four frames, each a separate file. Each new frame that arrives at the client replaces the old one, thereby giving the illusion of fluid movement.

The server and client make one connection that is open for as long as the CGI script runs. You can manually end a server push animation by clicking the browser's Stop button.

How Shockwave Works

Shockwave brings the next level of multimedia animation to the Web. Unlike client pull and server push, all of the timing and compiling of frames in a Shockwave animation is done before it reaches the Web.

1 The first step in a Shockwave animation happens in a multimedia authoring program such as Director or Authorware. An animation designer must gather the raw materials necessary for a short and compelling animation, such as still images, music, and sound effects.

Director™ Software by Macromedia

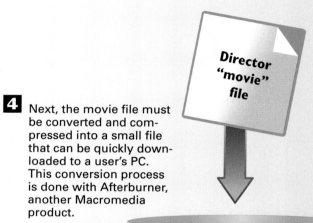

Director "movie" file

4 Next, the movie file must be converted and compressed into a small file that can be quickly downloaded to a user's PC. This conversion process is done with Afterburner, another Macromedia product.

Converts Director file to Shockwave file

Compress file

Timeline

frame 1   frame 2   frame 3

sound effect   sound effect

music

clickable button

stop

2 The authoring program then helps arrange the elements frame by frame along a time line. It also allows the designer to match a sound effect with a particular action in the animation.

Director "movie" file

3 When this step is done, the complete animation is saved as a Director or Authorware movie file.

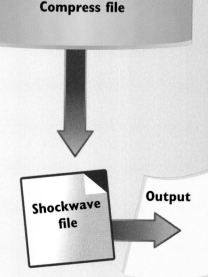

Shockwave file

Output

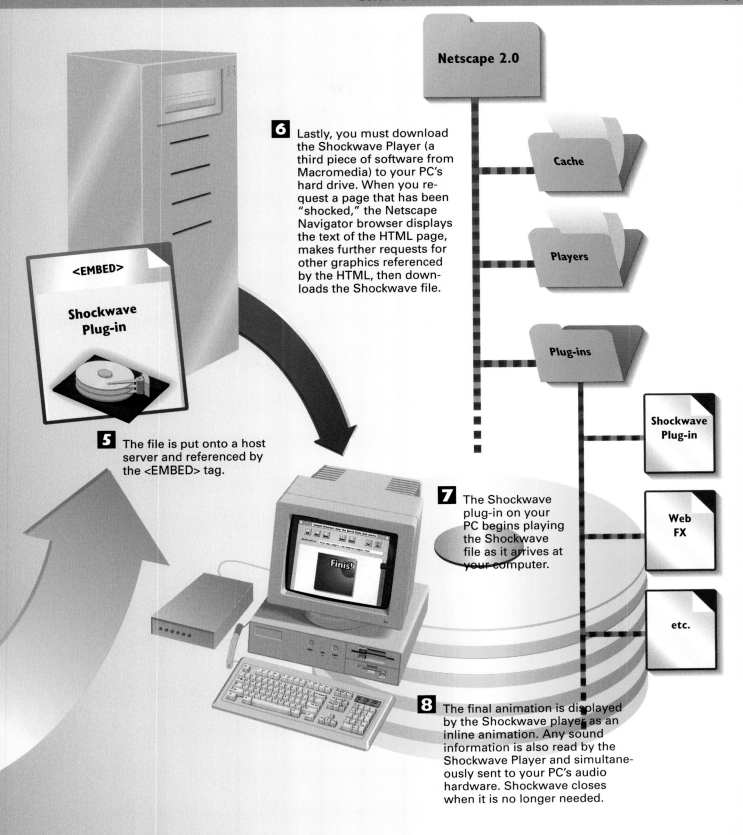

Netscape 2.0

Cache

Players

Plug-ins

Shockwave Plug-in

Web FX

etc.

6 Lastly, you must download the Shockwave Player (a third piece of software from Macromedia) to your PC's hard drive. When you request a page that has been "shocked," the Netscape Navigator browser displays the text of the HTML page, makes further requests for other graphics referenced by the HTML, then downloads the Shockwave file.

<EMBED>

Shockwave Plug-in

5 The file is put onto a host server and referenced by the <EMBED> tag.

7 The Shockwave plug-in on your PC begins playing the Shockwave file as it arrives at your computer.

Finis!

8 The final animation is displayed by the Shockwave player as an inline animation. Any sound information is also read by the Shockwave Player and simultaneously sent to your PC's audio hardware. Shockwave closes when it is no longer needed.

CHAPTER

15

How Java Works

JAVA is a programming language developed by Sun Microsystems for the World Wide Web. It is more powerful than simple text markup languages like HTML. Java, like other programming languages, contains commands to control the computer, but Java is tailored specifically for the Web. The Java language brings power to the Web in three revolutionary ways. First, the programs written in Java—called *applets*—are small, which means they can be downloaded quickly to your computer and used with great speed. Second, applets are cross-platform. The programs written in Java are sent over the Internet as raw code that is compiled by the client. Whatever operating system the client PC is using—including Windows 95, Macintosh, UNIX, and others—will be able to run the Java applet. Third and most important, applets are modular. This means various applets can be used together to make a larger program. For example, a word processor can be created from many little applets. One applet could display the text, another could check spelling, and still another could handle the print jobs. This is revolutionary because it all happens online. Imagine using such a word processor on the Web rather than a gigantic one on your computer's hard drive. You could use thousands of online applications for a specific job just once and still leave room for documents on your computer.

A common metaphor for the Internet is that it forms the world's largest hard drive by connecting thousands of smaller ones. If the Internet—and by extension the Web—is one big hard drive, then Java makes it into one big computer. This means that software previously available to one computer may now be available to thousands. Applets can travel over the Internet rather than live on an individual PC, which makes it available to any Java-capable computer linked to the Internet. Each of these applets loads and unloads only as needed; each is downloaded from the Internet if it does not already exist on the client computer; and each could be pieced together with any number of other applets to create a variety of larger applications such as spreadsheets and word processors.

It is possible to integrate dynamic media into a Web page using Java applets. Think of applets as mini-programs that have a single job, like playing a movie or animation. Imagine viewing a Web page that has moving text or buttons that are animated when clicked. One applet may be used to animate the button while another might be activated by that button.

In an animation written in Java, the entire file downloads to the browser before it starts running. For the Web server this is a distinct improvement over Netscape's server push technique. Animation with Java frees up the server for the next user. Plus, the animation loop looks smoother and more natural because the frames load faster from your local hard drive. Java can perform many other mixed-media functions currently executed by helper applications. It can play movies and sounds, and even take you through a VRML 3-D environment.

In addition, Java is completely cross-platform. This means that an applet written on a UNIX platform will work on a Macintosh or a Sun Sparc or any other kind of computer with a Java-capable client. By contrast, almost all helper applications are written specifically for one platform.

The Java programming language is very complicated. Luckily, there is a simpler Java interface called JavaScript. With JavaScript, you can have some control over ready-made applets created with the Java language. Imagine JavaScript as a car's steering, ignition, and gas and brake pedals, and Java as the nuts and bolts under the hood.

Java and JavaScript are not simply a replacement for helper apps. Theoretically, the sky is the limit on how Java is used. Applets can have virtually any purpose—from playing an animation to making mathematical calculations—that can easily exceed the functionality of CGI and helper applications used in today's Web pages. For Web developers and users alike, the only question that remains for such a powerful tool is not whether it will take the Web by storm, but how soon.

URLs of Note

News ticker is a Java applet: **http://www.cnet.com**

General Java information: **http://java.sun.com**

Applet examples: **http://www.ece.uc.edu/~franco/Java/javaapps.html**

More applet examples: **http://www.np.ac.sg:9080/~piaweb/class9/t4.html**

How Java Applets Work

There are three revolutionary ways in which the Java language brings power to the Web. Small Java programs known as applets can be downloaded quickly and used with great speed. Applets can also be used on a variety of computer platforms. Last, and most important, applets are modular. This means they can be used together to create a larger program.

1 A Java applet is called upon in an HTML document with the <APPLET> tag. When your browser reads this tag, the applet is downloaded from a server, just like graphic files and other media. The applet has a unique URL so it can easily be located by the browser.

Animation Applet

3 Once the applet arrives at the client, the client browser compiles the Java code and executes it within a specified part of the browser window. The actual screen size of the applet's display is dictated by commands within the <APPLET> tags. As you interact with the page, the applet continues to run. In many cases—such as animation—the applet will automatically restart itself when it reaches the end rather than quit. This process is called *looping*. Your browser software is responsible for displaying the whole Web page. The applet is responsible for the area used by the animation loop or other Java applet.

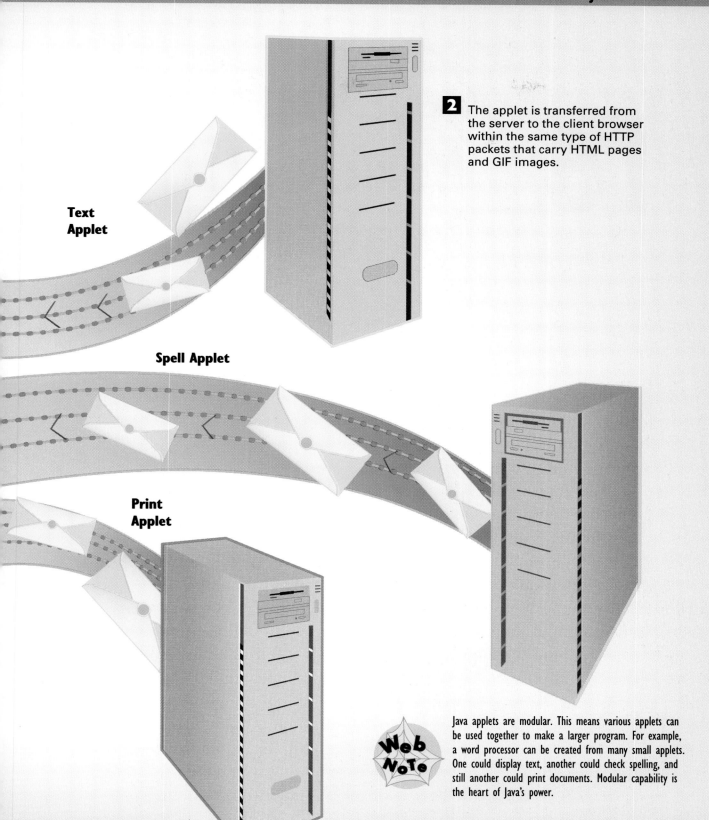

Text Applet

Spell Applet

Print Applet

2 The applet is transferred from the server to the client browser within the same type of HTTP packets that carry HTML pages and GIF images.

Java applets are modular. This means various applets can be used together to make a larger program. For example, a word processor can be created from many small applets. One could display text, another could check spelling, and still another could print documents. Modular capability is the heart of Java's power.

CHAPTER

16

How Web Sites Work with Databases

ONE of the most useful applications of the Web these days is to link a Web site with a database so that Web surfers can search for specific information. Of course this makes great sense: If the Web is more or less a distributed database of documents, why not use the Web to access other databases, too? In essence, the Web page becomes the *front end* of the database applications, enabling you to select search criteria and execute even complex searches of a database that resides on the host computer. And just as the Web can serve up data, it can collect it, too. Many Web sites, for example, ask users to "register" their names, addresses, and other demographic information—data that is captured and stored in a database.

A well-known and widely used example of this link between Web site and database is the popular Yahoo! Web site. The Yahoo! site serves as a front end to an extensive database of Web site descriptions, which can be searched according to keywords. The welcome page includes a search dialog box in which you enter a keyword that represents the subject matter you are looking for. Selecting "search" from the page sends a request from the browser to the Web server to bring back a list of all Web sites that contain your keyword.

Many companies are using this approach to make their resources available directly to customers. Federal Express, for example, uses the Web to give customers access to package tracking records. By entering a package's airbill number into the search field of the Web page, you launch a query of the FedEx tracking database to find out where your package is in the shipping company's courier network. If the package was delivered to its destination, the database results tell you when the package arrived and who signed for it.

This example shows just how powerful a Web-based database search can be. The package tracking database is the heart of FedEx's shipping service. Before the Web, customers called a customer service representative who conducted the search from a desktop computer, and relayed the answer over the phone. By making the database available directly to customers, FedEx has saved thousands of dollars in customer support costs.

But how does this all work? You don't have to be a corporate giant—or for that matter even an able programmer—to link your Web site to a database. In fact, linking a Web site to a database can be relatively simple. The database can take just about any form, and can be as simple as a FileMaker Pro database, or as complex as an Oracle SQL database. The Web site is more or less like any other site; in fact, most Web-driven databases start out as ordinary Web sites and evolve to include an attached database. The bridge that brings Web site and database together is the Common Gateway Interface (CGI).

On the client side of the database, you see a Web page that includes a form in which you enter your search terms. By executing the search, you launch a CGI script that sends a search command to the Web server in the form of a link to the CGI bin on the Web server. This URL is somewhat different from the URLs we discussed earlier because within it is embedded your search criteria. So a search on the Yahoo site for public relations firms looks like this:

```
http://search.yahoo.com/bin/search?p=public+relations
```

When the Web server receives this URL, it identifies the URL as a trigger for a CGI script—in this example, called "search"—and passes it along with the search criteria—"public relations" in this example—to the mini-program using the Common Gateway Interface. The CGI script then sends the search to the database, receives the results of the query, along with the HTML page created by the database to contain the result, and passes it on to the Web server to be sent back to the client. That's a lot of handing off of requests and data, but typically even a search of a large database is very fast, because most UNIX and Windows NT databases—the types most often used—can perform these tasks simultaneously. (For more on CGI, see Chapter 10.)

Databases are a very efficient way to deliver lots of information to people. Without a database, the Webmaster would need to anticipate every search that visitors to the site might want, and compose individual pages that included information. With a database, the Webmaster provides a search page, and the resulting HTML pages are generated on the fly.

URLs of Note

Yahoo! is a popular database of sites on the World Wide Web. Each Web site is indexed by keyword, according to the name of the Web page and a brief description of the content of the site. In addition to serving as a good example of a databased Web site, Yahoo! contains a page of listings for Web database tool developers—a good place to start your search for more information: **http://www.yahoo.com/**

Federal Express demonstrates just how useful Web access to a corporate database can be. On this site, FedEx customers can search by their airbill number to track the location of their packages: **http://www.fedex.com/**

The following Web site, by the author of *Building Internet Database Servers with CGI,* is a great place to learn more about this topic: **http://cscsun1.larc.nasa.gov/~beowolf/db/web_access.html**

How the Web Works with Databases

The Web makes an effective front end to databases, enabling users to search for and receive just the information they are looking for.

1 The search begins on a Web page that includes a form field to accept search terms and HTML codes to execute a CGI script. The browser may pass the data to the Web server in a query string. The query string contains the name of the CGI script in a directory called cgi-bin. This directory is followed by a subdirectory that includes the search terms, often separated by a question mark or slashes. The HTML code for an extra path might look like this: `<a href="cgi-bin/search/matt/fish/">`.

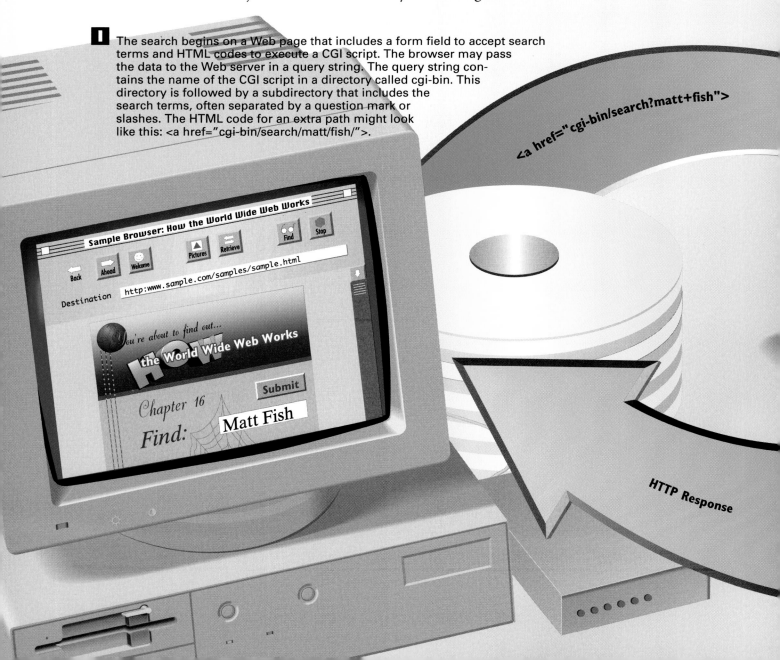

2 When the Web server receives the URL with the embedded search terms, it sends the information through the CGI program—typically stored in a unique directory that contains all the CGI scripts serviced by the Web server—to the database.

To CGI

From CGI

Database Server

directory/cgi/subdirectory

Name-First	Name-Last
Erin	
Lars	Fish
Matt	Fish
Patrick	Fish
	Fish

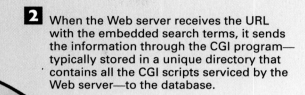

You're about to find out...
the World Wide Web Works

Chapter 16

Hi, I'm Matt Fish...

3 The database retrieves the record or records that match the search criteria. The database record may contain text and numeric data, as well as references to graphics or other data types.

4 The database returns the data to the Web server via CGI in the form of a new HTML page. The server then sends the page back to the client browser as a new HTML page.

CHAPTER

17

Discovering Internet Relay Chat on the Web

WHILE not exclusively the province of the Web, Internet Relay Chat, or IRC, lets people from all across the Internet join in real-time conversations. Because of the Web, more and more people are discovering IRC. If you've spent any time on commercial online services such as America Online and CompuServe, you know that one of their appeals is the ability to "chat" with other members of the service. When you enter a chat area on America Online, for example, anything you type and send to the network can be seen by anyone else who is in that same chat area, and vice versa. In this way, you can "talk" with other people who also use the service.

Chat rooms create a sense of community that often seems missing from the Web. You can browse from site to site, and usually you feel you're surfing on your own. Except for occasional delays caused by heavy traffic on a particular site, you don't have a sense that anyone else is on the Web with you. There *is* a way to talk to other people on the Internet, though, and it's called *Internet Relay Chat.*

The IRC protocol is a text-based conferencing system developed by Jarkko Iokarinen in the late 1980s. Like other communications on the Web, IRC uses the TCP/IP protocol in a client/server model. In a typical setup, a single server acts as the central "meeting" point to which clients or other servers connect in order to create the IRC network. The server manages the conversation, transferring the dialog to the various clients connected to the server. Software at the client end of the connection is used to connect to the IRC server and to send and receive chat dialog. One popular IRC client software program is called ircII, and like many other Internet tools, the IRC software is incorporated in the Web browsing software. In order to be recognized by the server, each client must have a unique *nickname* of up to nine characters in length, and must also provide the name of the computer from which they are connecting, their real user name, and the name of the server to which the client is connected.

To create an IRC network, one or more clients must form a *channel,* which is simply a named group of one or more clients who all receive messages passed through that channel. The channel is created when the first client joins it and it is dissolved when the last client leaves. So that some order is maintained within an IRC network, one client is designated as the *operator.* The operator (also known as the "channel operator," "chop," or "chanop") "owns" the channel and has the power to manage the discussion, which includes kicking out people who become obnoxious or otherwise disrupt the flow of discussion.

An appropriate metaphor for IRC is the CB radio made popular in the 1970s. Radio operators who are tuned in to the same channel can hear and speak to one another. The same is true for IRC except that it works in text. The client connects to an Internet Relay Network, or server.

To be heard, the client needs to join a channel. To do so, you would type **/list** to see all the names of all the channels currently available on that server. Some channels are preceded with the # symbol to denote that they are global channels available to anyone across the Internet, with the conversation handed off from server to server across the Net. Other channels have the prefix &, which denotes that the channel is only available to people connected directly to that particular server. To join a channel, you type **/join** followed by the name of the channel. Once on the channel, any comment you type is sent across the channel and everyone on the channel can see it.

You choose a nickname, or nick, to use while you're engaged in IRC. To do this, you type **/nick <nickname>**, where the enclosed text is the name you intend to use. You can also send private messages to a person using their nickname. This is done by entering **/msg <nick>** (where nick is the name of the person you want to send the message to) followed by your message.

If it's not already obvious, the slash (/) at the beginning of a line indicates an IRC command. (One good command to know is /help.) Any line that does not begin with the slash is assumed to be a message and is sent to the entire channel, unless you specify a particular nickname to receive the message. IRC messages are in simple ASCII text, in lines of up to 510 characters followed by a carriage return and a line feed.

There are plenty of places on the Web to learn more about IRC and to find listings of sites that conduct IRC discussions. A good place to start is the Web site at http://www2.undernet.org:8080/~cs93jtl/IRC.html/.

But as important as it is to understand how IRC works, it's more important to understand "netiquette," the etiquette of how to behave when you are on the Net. The key is to be considerate of other people on the channel. When you join a channel, don't greet everyone individually; all those "hello's" just bog down the system. Observe the conversation that's in progress and comment appropriately; asking "What's everyone talking about?" is annoying to others who are in mid-discussion. And one sure way to get kicked off a channel is to harass people by hurling insults, name calling, or otherwise provoking people.

Remember that IRC isn't a secure method of communication. Messages you send are passed along over the IRC network from server to server between you and the people who you are talking to, even when you're sending someone a so-called private message. Any server administrator along the path could capture and log IRC comments that pass over his or her server. A word to the wise: Don't say anything over IRC that's confidential.

While most people think of IRC as a virtual coffee klatch, the protocol can be used in a variety of practical ways. In fact, IRC took off during the Gulf War, as people used the Internet to stay in touch with family and friends serving in the conflict. IRC has been used to create virtual classrooms, where instructors "lecture" to a group of people connected to the same IRC channel. Groups can hold meetings via IRC, and it's even been used to "stage" theatrical performances.

As you explore the world of IRC, you'll find that the topics are as varied as the people who participate. People from around the world discuss politics, technology, world events, culture— just about anything you can imagine. And while most discussions are conducted in English, it's not unusual to find IRCs happening in other languages, including German, Japanese, French, and Finnish—the land where IRC got started. The most important thing is to jump in and explore.

URLS of Note

Here's a great place to start learning more about Internet Relay Chat via the Web:
http://www2.undernet.org:8080/2cs93jtl/IRC.html/

The following Web site is a nice example of a site that has added chat. Here, people can "talk" about music: **http://www.ffly.com/**

How Internet Relay Chat Works

Internet Relay Chat lets people hold real-time conferences across the Internet. As a multimedia subset of the Net, the Web is an effective vehicle for introducing surfers to IRC. Like the Web's HTTP, the IRC protocol builds on the TCP/IP protocol, using a client/server architecture. At the client end, the user employs IRC client software, such as ircII or software integrated into a Web browser to connect to an IRC server.

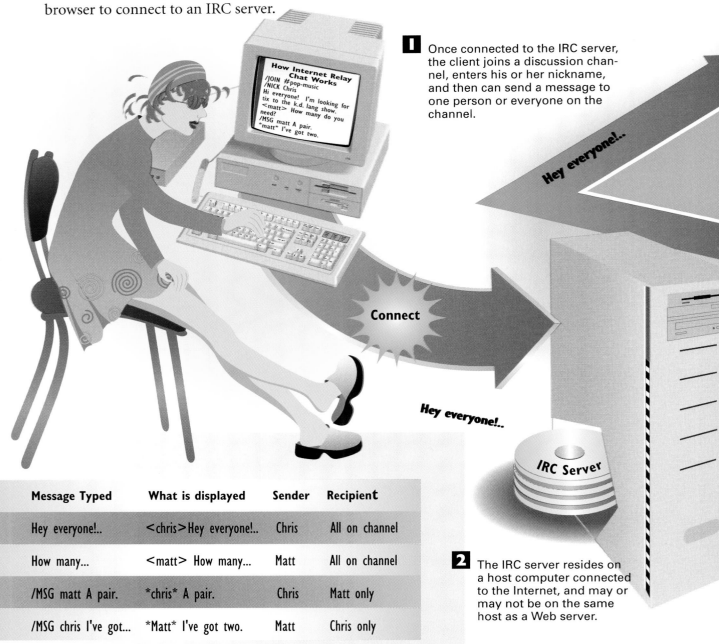

1 Once connected to the IRC server, the client joins a discussion channel, enters his or her nickname, and then can send a message to one person or everyone on the channel.

How Internet Relay
Chat Works
/JOIN #pop-music
/NICK Chris
Hi everyone! I'm looking for
tix to the k.d. lang show.
<matt> How many do you
need?
/MSG matt A pair.
matt I've got two.

Hey everyone!..

Connect

Hey everyone!..

IRC Server

2 The IRC server resides on a host computer connected to the Internet, and may or may not be on the same host as a Web server.

Message Typed	What is displayed	Sender	Recipient
Hey everyone!..	<chris>Hey everyone!..	Chris	All on channel
How many...	<matt> How many...	Matt	All on channel
/MSG matt A pair.	*chris* A pair.	Chris	Matt only
/MSG chris I've got...	*Matt* I've got two.	Matt	Chris only

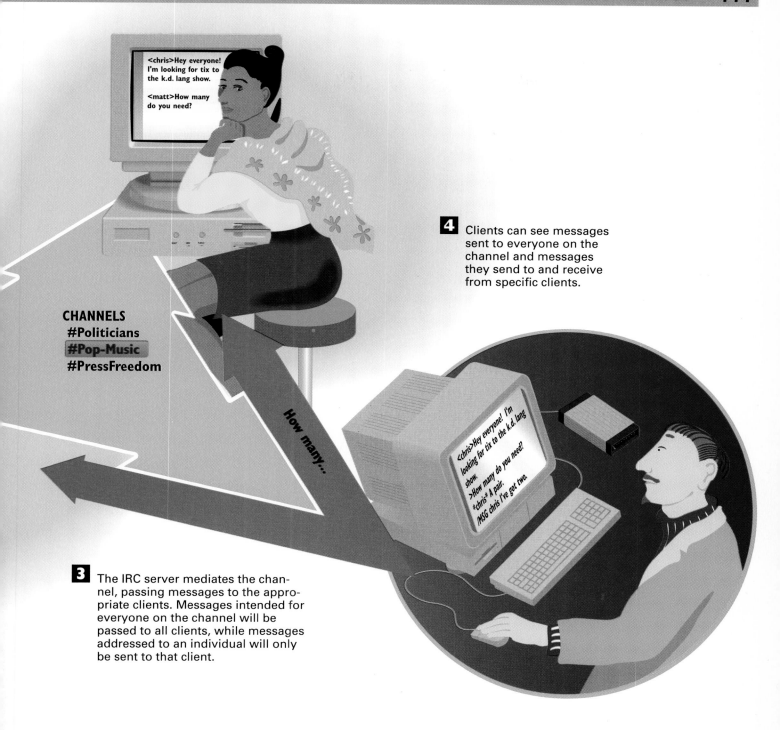

CHANNELS
#Politicians
#Pop-Music
#PressFreedom

4 Clients can see messages sent to everyone on the channel and messages they send to and receive from specific clients.

3 The IRC server mediates the channel, passing messages to the appropriate clients. Messages intended for everyone on the channel will be passed to all clients, while messages addressed to an individual will only be sent to that client.

Use some caution when participating in an IRC. If someone asks you to enter a cryptic command, don't do so unless you're absolutely sure you know what the command is and who's asking you to enter it. Some commands in the IRC client give control of your client software to others on the IRC network.

CHAPTER

18

Making Phone Calls on the Web

THROUGHOUT this book, we've talked about how the Internet relies in large measure on the world's telecommunications infrastructure in order for computers on the Internet to connect to one another. With computers on the Internet already using the telephone network, among other systems, to communicate, it takes only a short leap of the imagination to think about using the Internet as a telephone service—and that's exactly what's happening. With the right computer hardware, specialty software or Web browser add-on program, and an Internet connection, you can speak in real time over the Internet just as you would talk on a phone. Internet telephone service, also known as *audio conferencing*, isn't unique to the Web. Many people, however, are learning about the idea from their use of the Web, and are making Internet telephone calls from Web browser-based software or browser applets.

Audio conferencing is a fairly straightforward proposition: As you talk, your voice is digitized and this digital data is sent in TCP/IP packets across the Internet. In effect, voice data is transmitted just like an e-mail message, a Web page, or an electronic file. When it reaches its destination, the digital data is reassembled and converted back to analog sound and heard over speakers or a headset attached to the computer's sound cord. The trick is compressing the voice data so that the digitized files are small enough to send efficiently across the Internet while maintaining its sound quality. A 14.4 kbps modem connection—the slowest speed at which audio conferencing is reliable—sends and receives a theoretical maximum of 1,800 bytes of data each second. Non-compressed telephone-quality speech requires 8,000 bytes per second of bandwidth. One solution, of course, would be to get more communications bandwidth—not a practical idea for dial-up Internet customers who are connecting at 28.8 kbps. The better solution is to compress the digital audio, transmit it, and decompress it at the other end. Effectively, this packs more sound information into fewer bytes, though some sound quality is lost in the process.

A number of methods are being used to encode and compress audio data. Some audio conferencing software programs rely on proprietary methods to handle audio data compression. As a result, those who use these programs can communicate only with other people who use the same software. Other programs have adopted standard data compression protocols. The standardized protocol most often used is GSM (Global System for Mobile telecommunications), a protocol suite used widely in Europe for digital cellular communications. The advantage of using an accepted protocol is compatibility: Programs that use one of these standards can talk to any other program that uses the same standard. While the GSM system is already in use, Microsoft and Intel have also announced their plans to work together to devise an Internet telephone standard, and Netscape has announced plans to include audio-conferencing capabilities in its Navigator release 3.0.

The sound quality of an Internet telephone conversation can vary, depending on a number of factors. Perhaps the biggest impact on quality is the bandwidth of the connection to the Internet itself. Those who connect to the Internet across a corporate network, then through a T1 line, may actually find that their Internet telephone conversation is clearer than a phone call through a local phone company. POTS—plain old telephone service—uses analog signals and is also subject to significant line "noise." Those with dial-up access via a local Internet service provider will find that, if the line is clear, the quality will be reasonably good.

Of course, you'll want a fast modem to take advantage of that clean line. A 14.4 kbps modem is the absolute minimum for a dial-up connection and a 28.8 kbps modem will work well with most audio conferencing applications. The speed of your modem is important, but so is the speed of your computer. You'll want a 486 PC or a speedy Macintosh or Power Macintosh, because audio conferencing relies on the client processor to decompress and reconvert the digital audio back to analog signals before it is heard. Your PC also needs a sound card, speakers, and a microphone to provide the equivalent parts of an analog "telephone" setup.

With the hardware in place, the only other variable is the software you choose to handle the audio processing. This may sound like a trivial choice, but it's not. There are a dozen or more programs available both commercially in software stores and as free applications downloadable from the Internet. The choice you make will depend on the features you want.

All audio conferencing software lets you have a conversation with one individual, but some programs also include *multicasting* capabilities that enable you to conduct a conversation with several people at different Internet addresses. This is done using the MBone, or "Multicast Backbone," that allows one host site to broadcast data to many client locations. MBone is used for text chat (discussed in Chapter 17) and for streaming audio broadcasts (talked about in Chapter 13), as well as for voice conferencing.

You'll also consider whether you want, need, or can get *half* or *full duplex conversations*. Half duplex permits only one person to be heard at a time. Typically, you click an icon or press a key to speak. The other person hears you, then responds. If both people try to speak at the same time, neither will be heard. A full duplex conversation lets you speak and hear at the same time, and is more like a traditional telephone conversation. Full duplex sounds are ideal, but some slower computers, and Internet connections will not support full duplex. Check your sound card documentation or call the manufacturer to be sure your card supports full duplex mode.

The final significant consideration in choosing audio conferencing software is whether it will enable you to have Internet voice conferences. So long as your software supports the same techniques for connecting and for compressing audio as the software used by the people you want to call, you should not experience compatibility problems. To ensure this, both you and the person you wish to speak with can use the same software, but that's not absolutely necessary. Many audio conferencing programs have adopted VAT (the first voice conferencing program for UNIX) and RTP (Real Time Protocol) as compatible standards for establishing audio conference connections. VAT and RTP are compatible, but RTP includes ways to control the quality of the sound. Audio conferencing programs such as Maven, Netphone, VAT, and Speak Freely support VAT and RTP. GSM is becoming the standard for audio compression and is also supported by Maven, NetPhone, and Speak Freely, among others.

There are dozens of audio conferencing programs and audio conferencing browsers, but we're unable to discuss them all here. Still, the ones described below will give you a head start in learning more about the available programs and choosing one to fit your needs.

Maven, the first audio conferencing program for the Mac, is available free but it needs at least a 28.8 kbps modem to deliver its good sound quality. The software can be downloaded at ftp://sunsite.unc.edu/pub/packages/infosystems/maven or ftp://ftp.univie.ac.at/systems/mac/info-mac/comm/tcp/.

NetPhone requires less bandwidth than Maven so it works over slower modems, but the sound quality isn't as good. A free Mac-compatible demo that limits conversations to 90 seconds is available at http://www.emagic.com/.

CoolTalk brings telephone capabilities to version 3.0 of the Netscape Navigator Web browser. Netscape claims the sound quality rivals that of a regular phone conversation. A downloadable version of the new browser is available at http://home.netscape.com/.

Internet Phone is a layer on top of Internet Relay Chat, which lets you easily find other people to talk to. It uses proprietary encoding and compression techniques so you can talk only with other Mac and Windows Internet Phone users. A free demo and more information is available at http://www.vocaltec.com/.

CU-SeeMe, a project at Cornell University, provides both audio *and* video conferencing capabilities. To take the best advantage of both the sound and video you will need at least a 28.8 kbps modem connection. In addition to its good audio and the extra benefit of video, CU-SeeMe is one of the more widely compatible audio conferencing applications for Windows and Macintosh computers. For more information, see http://cu-seeme.cornell.edu/.

Speak Freely is aptly named: The program is free and gives users lots of voice-related capabilities, including voice mail, multicasting, and good sound quality. Currently, you can use this only to speak to other Speak Freely users. For more information contact http://www.fourmilab.ch/netfone/windows/speak_freely.html/.

WebPhone, developed by Internet Telephone Company, supports GSM compression and has a host of features including voice mail, Web integration, and multiple lines for simultaneous conversations. More information is available at http://www.itelco.com/.

WebTalk, from Quarterdeck, is a Web-integrated audio conferencing program that offers good sound quality, and supports a variety of compression techniques. Information is available at http://www.qdeck.com/qdeck/press/webphone.html.

In this chapter, we've talked about using the Internet to "call" people at other Internet addresses. Know that there are a number of experimental projects in the works, one of which, called Free World Dialup, allows people using Internet Phone to make calls from regular phone lines to regular phone service customers using a phone gateway. This gateway is similar to an e-mail gateway discussed in Chapter 1, and passes the digitized audio from the TCP/IP network over to the telephone network. For more information on Free World Dialup, you can join a mailing list discussion by sending e-mail to majordomo@pulver.com. Include the text "subscribe free-world-dialup@pulver.com" in the body of the e-mail message.

URLs of Note

The Internet Telephony page provides up-to-date information about audio conferencing on the Internet: **http://rpcp.mit.edu/~asears/main.html/**

MediaCast uses Internet broadcast technology to deliver information to audiences around the Net. This page offers links to more information about the technologies it uses: **http://www.mediacast.com/MediaCast/Instructions.html/**

The Multicast Backbone distributes real-time audio to clients on the Internet: **http://www.northcoast.com/savetz/mbone/toc.html/**

The Global System for Mobile telecommunications is an emerging standard for audio conferencing: **http://www.cs.tu-berline.de/toast.html/**

How Internet Audio Conferencing Works

Clients running audio conferencing software can talk to one another in real time, so long as they are using software that supports the same techniques for connecting and for compressing digital audio data.

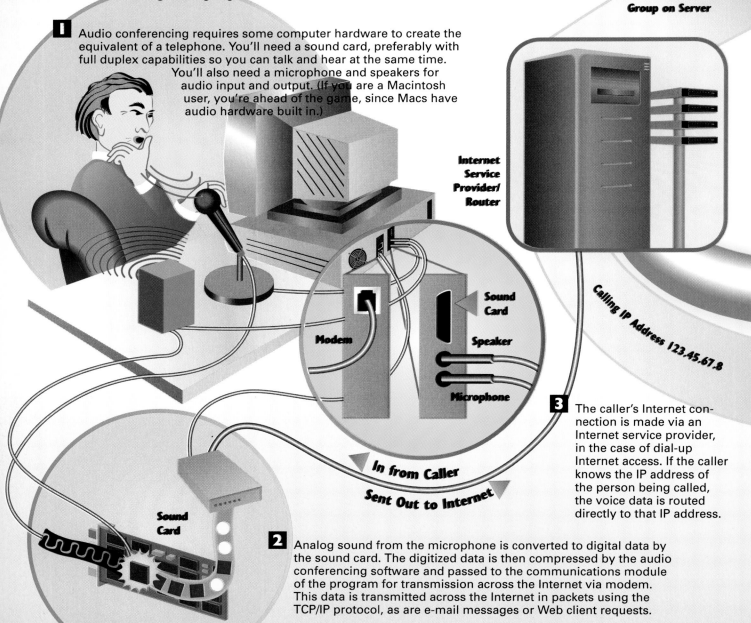

1 Audio conferencing requires some computer hardware to create the equivalent of a telephone. You'll need a sound card, preferably with full duplex capabilities so you can talk and hear at the same time. You'll also need a microphone and speakers for audio input and output. (If you are a Macintosh user, you're ahead of the game, since Macs have audio hardware built in.)

Conference to Group on Server

Internet Service Provider/ Router

Calling IP Address 123.45.67.8

Sound Card

Modem

Speaker

Microphone

In from Caller

Sent Out to Internet

Sound Card

3 The caller's Internet connection is made via an Internet service provider, in the case of dial-up Internet access. If the caller knows the IP address of the person being called, the voice data is routed directly to that IP address.

2 Analog sound from the microphone is converted to digital data by the sound card. The digitized data is then compressed by the audio conferencing software and passed to the communications module of the program for transmission across the Internet via modem. This data is transmitted across the Internet in packets using the TCP/IP protocol, as are e-mail messages or Web client requests.

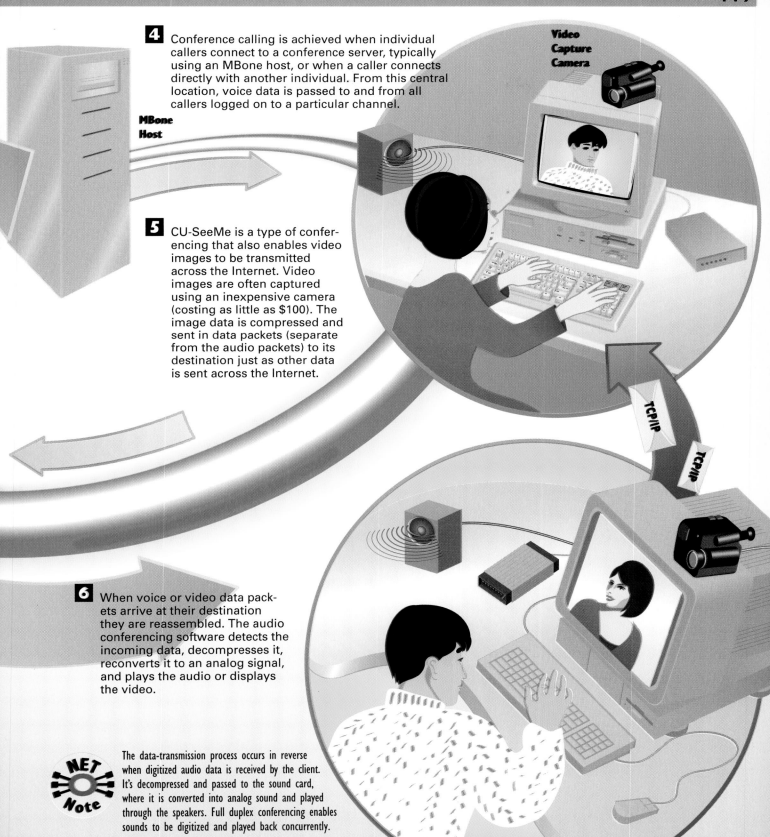

4 Conference calling is achieved when individual callers connect to a conference server, typically using an MBone host, or when a caller connects directly with another individual. From this central location, voice data is passed to and from all callers logged on to a particular channel.

MBone Host

Video Capture Camera

5 CU-SeeMe is a type of conferencing that also enables video images to be transmitted across the Internet. Video images are often captured using an inexpensive camera (costing as little as $100). The image data is compressed and sent in data packets (separate from the audio packets) to its destination just as other data is sent across the Internet.

TCP/IP

TCP/IP

6 When voice or video data packets arrive at their destination they are reassembled. The audio conferencing software detects the incoming data, decompresses it, reconverts it to an analog signal, and plays the audio or displays the video.

NET Note

The data-transmission process occurs in reverse when digitized audio data is received by the client. It's decompressed and passed to the sound card, where it is converted into analog sound and played through the speakers. Full duplex conferencing enables sounds to be digitized and played back concurrently.

CHAPTER

19

The Web Goes 3-D

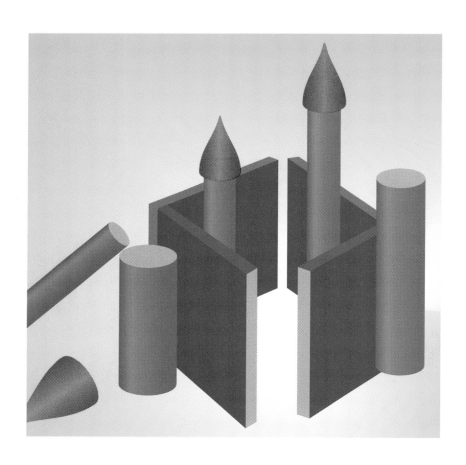

As technology advances, Web pages are becoming more sophisticated visually. Gone are the days when text-only Web browsers were the standard. Now sound, animation, video, and 3-D are regularly included. Yet 3-D can mean different things on the Web. In some cases images may have a three-dimensional look, but no usable third dimension. Many Web sites have graphics that only appear to be 3-D. For example, a still picture of a ball may use light and shadow to give it a spherical look. Or a page may use navigational buttons that stand in relief from the two-dimensional surface of the page. These examples only look three-dimensional. They are drawn in a 2-D environment using light and shadow techniques. The only way to navigate around such images is to scroll left and right or up and down.

Virtual Reality, or VR, takes the user into the third dimension. A virtual reality site actually allows you to navigate in the three-dimensional space. Not to be confused with a 3-D movie, a VR Web site will not neccessarily jump out at you like the shark in *Jaws III*. Instead, VR gives you new ways to navigate virtual space. A user can go left and right, up and down, forward and backward. Some VR controllers let you "fly" through virtual space or "walk" on virtual ground.

VRML (virtual reality modeling language) is the most common language used on the Web to create VR worlds. A modeling language is simply a mathematical description of simple geometric shapes. For instance, the mathematical expression for a cube is described by the length, width, and height of a cube and the relationship of each to the other. A VRML programmer creates VR "worlds" by putting together various geometric shapes into a three-dimensional model. A virtual castle, for example, can be built by combining different size cubes, pyramids, cones, and spheres into a model. Later, two-dimensional textures and colors are applied to the surfaces of the 3-D model, giving it a realistic look and feel. When you navigate these VR worlds, the geometric shapes represent solid objects that you can manipulate.

Currently, the only way to look at VR worlds is to download a VRML browser or a plug-in for a standard Web browser. A VR plug-in will automatically display pages written in VRML, much like a helper application plays a sound or movie. A VRML Web page is transferred like any other text or image file over the Internet. It goes from server to client via TCP/IP and HTTP packets. Once the code for a page arrives at your local PC, the browser reads the document's MIME type and either displays it (if it is a special VR browser) or hands it to the appropriate VR software or plug-in to display. The VR software translates the mathematical modeling information into a display within the browser window. Many VR plug-ins also provide you with additional navigation controls that help you move all directions in 3-D space.

Much of the fun of VR is being able interact with the sites and "live" in the worlds. Although they may run slowly, try out a few sites yourself and see what's out (or in) there. Many VRML sites are Java-enhanced, which means more objects move just like in the real world. You are always the center of a VR world because your point of view is always displayed, much like looking through a scuba mask underwater. If these computer-generated worlds are cleverly designed—and if you have a fast enough connection to the Web—the VR experience can be very cool indeed.

URLs of Note

Squirrel Virtual Reality—about 20 VRML worlds to explore: **http://www.squirrel.com.au/virtualreality/vrworlds.html**

Terminal Reality—virtual airport: **http://www.zdnet.com/~zdi/vrml/airport.html**

TerraVirtua—an excellent source for VRML information including some VRML worlds: **http://www.terravirtua.com/**

VRML-o-Rama!: **http://www.well.com/user/spidaman/vrml.html**

The VRML Foundry—a guide to VRML tutorials, converters, browsers, and other resources: **http://www.mcp.com/general/foundry/**

How Virtual Reality and VRML Work

A modeling language is a mathematical explanation of basic geometric shapes. VRML (virtual reality modeling language) is the most common language used to create VR worlds on the Web.

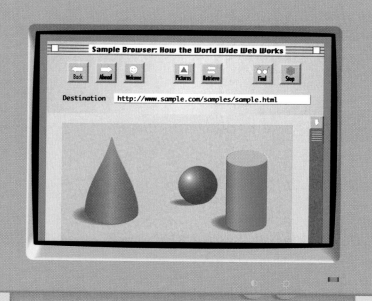

```
ShapeHints {
        vertexOrdering CLOCKWISE
        shapeType SOLID
}
Material {
        ambientColor 0.080125801 0.0821575 0.145455
        diffuseColor  0.33051899 0.2289 0.600000002
        specularColor  0.29090899 0.29090899 0.29090899
        emissiveColor  0 0 0
        shininess          0.78787899
        transparency    0
}
Coordinate3 {
    point   [0 900 700,
            700 900 700,
            700 900 0,
            0 900 0,
            700 0 0,
            700 0 700,
            0 0 700,
            0 0 0]
```

1 Web developers use VRML authoring software to create virtual worlds. First, a developer draws 3-D shapes needed for a virtual object, and a *geometry translator* changes the shapes back into the mathematical formulas of VRML.

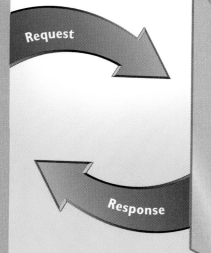

Sample Browser: How the World Wide Web Works

Back | Ahead | Welcome | Pictures | Retrieve | Find | Stop

Destination http://www.sample.com/samples/sample.html

Request

Response

2 Next, the developer arranges a model in a virtual 3-D space that simulates actual space. He or she uses the basic geometric shapes—such as pyramids, cones, cubes, and spheres—created in step 1. Imagine playing with a child's doll house and arranging blocks, balls, and cones inside each room. Now imagine a tiny camera taking photos of the room from every possible angle. This is what VRML does mathematically so users can view virtual objects from all sides.

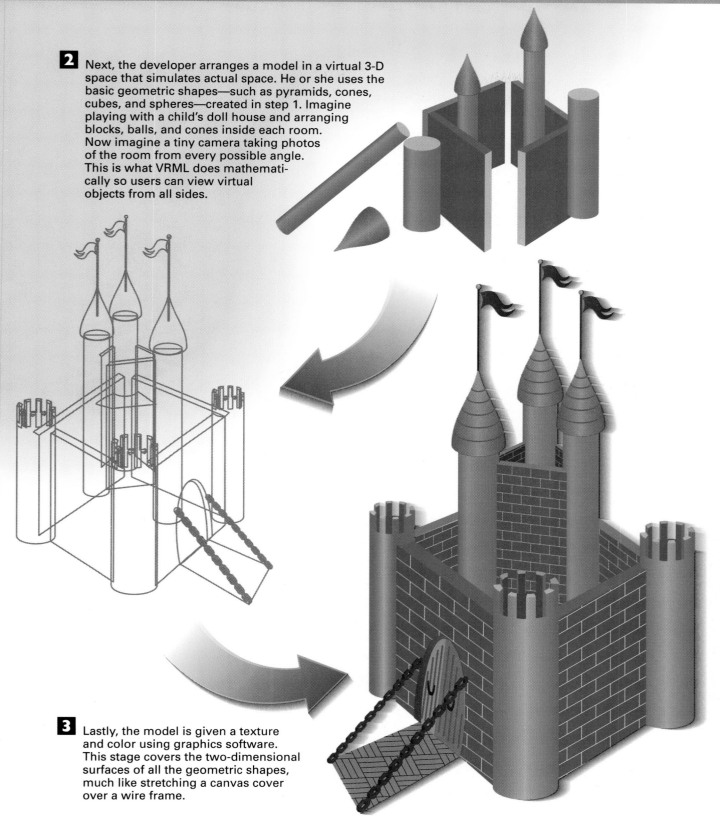

3 Lastly, the model is given a texture and color using graphics software. This stage covers the two-dimensional surfaces of all the geometric shapes, much like stretching a canvas cover over a wire frame.

P A R T

PUTTING THE WEB TO WORK

IN the first three parts of this book we've talked about the architecture of the Web, the telecommunications infrastructure and protocols that make it work, and the emerging multimedia technologies that are making the Web the most exciting publishing media to come along since television. In this section, though, it's time to get down to work.

The Web is only as valuable as the uses it's put to, so here we'll discuss the technologies that are turning the Web into a viable "place" for commerce and communications.

The Web, for example, is becoming a thriving shopping mall. These days, it's hard to find something you *can't* buy on the Web using "cyber cash" or "secure" credit card transmissions to pay the tab. Of course, you don't want some hack to pick up your credit card number as it is sent across the Net. A handful of companies are creating encryption techniques and other payment systems to secure these transactions.

Corporations are finding the Web a valuable communications tool, enabling them to communicate directly with their customers. But having thousands of people accessing corporate computers poses certain security risks. A company may want people to get into their computer to retrieve certain information, but not want them poking around in confidential corporate systems. That's where firewalls and other security measures come in. These systems enable the public to access the company computer for certain information, but create a boundary so that the public can't get to private data.

If protecting companies from snooping eyes is a corporate concern, protecting youngsters from "adult" content is perhaps a greater social and parental concern. While the bulk of material published on the Web is suitable for audiences of all ages, there is some content that may be considered for mature audiences only. As more and more children are surfing the Web, parents are looking for ways to limit their children's access to this adult material. We'll discuss some of these methods in Chapter 22.

Perhaps this book has inspired you to create your own Web page. Thousands of people have gotten the bug and are using their memberships in commercial online services to create their own Web pages. That's one starting point, but more robust Web sites will require you to set up shop on your own server or on an access provider's server. It's not hard to do, and we'll take you through the steps to build and post your own Web page in Chapter 23.

Finally, a new term is emerging as companies are discovering that the same infrastructure that lets them communicate outside the company is a great tool to communicate within the organization. These organizations have coined the term *intranet* to refer to internal use of the Web architecture, and as we bring this book to a close, we'll talk about how these internal Web sites differ from those on the broader Internet.

So now, let's get down to work.

CHAPTER

20

Shopping on the Web

THE Web is a great place to give and get information, and when that information is about products, it only makes sense to be able to complete the transaction when you find something you want to buy. But how does merchandise get paid for when the customer is sitting at a computer at home or in the office and the "store" is a Web site that may originate from anywhere in the world?

The obvious answer is to use a credit card, just as you would if you were buying something over the telephone. But the Internet may not be a private or secure place to exchange information, so it's understandable that people are unwilling to expose their credit card or other personal financial information to this network. The fear is that data capture programs on routing computers might grab credit card numbers as they are passed across the Internet on their way from the client to the destination host computer.

To combat this threat, dozens of organizations, including the major credit card companies, automated finance services, and Internet and Web standards-setting bodies, are developing schemes to provide secure, encrypted financial transactions over the Internet. The challenge is significant; developing a scheme that can't be hacked is tough work. The payoff is potentially huge. The Web alone represents a tremendous opportunity to create an efficient worldwide electronic marketplace, enabling people to buy goods and services from vendors as diverse as name-brand mail order companies like Lands' End and Eddie Bauer and mom-and-pop retailers who without the Web would be unable to make their products widely available.

The schemes for secure transactions take two general approaches. One approach encrypts personal financial information, such as credit card numbers, so that it can be transferred across the Internet in a manner that would not let prying eyes read the data. The second method creates a system of "cyber-dollars," electronic credits that only authorized merchants can redeem for real money. The former is most convenient and more likely to be widely accepted by consumers, although it is also the method most vulnerable to hackers.

We could fill an entire book with the issues surrounding electronic commerce and the techniques being used to ensure that consumers can safely and conveniently purchase the goods and services they discover when shopping the Web marketplace. The illustrations on the following pages describe some of the techniques developed by organizations leading this campaign. They are offered here as examples, rather than endorsements of the technology, and they are the systems that consumers are most likely to encounter when they take a shopping trip on the Web. Recognize, though, that these standards are evolving and new and even more secure techniques may supersede today's best efforts.

Credit card encryption scenarios have been put forth by companies such as VeriFone, CyberCash, and Checkfree—and by credit card giants VISA and MasterCard, who have agreed to work together to develop an Internet encryption standard. These schemes work by placing an electronic payment helper application at the client end of the transaction, and a verification system at the merchant end of the line. The helper app or encryption-enabled browser encrypts the user's credit card information and sends the secured data to the merchant. In turn, the merchant passes the payment information to a processing center that decrypts the credit card information, verifies it, and uses an existing private and secured data communications network to authorize payment from the credit card company to the merchant. In most cases, this means of securing, verifying, and authorizing payment relies on the same secure financial networks used to handle point-of-purchase credit card payments—just as if you used your credit card to make a purchase at a store.

In addition to these secured credit card transactions, a number of companies are working on electronic or "cyber-dollar" scenarios that will enable consumers to purchase goods and services anonymously. That is, the consumer uses the digital equivalent of paper currency to make purchases and need not provide personal information (such as credit card or bank information) to do so. Using this method of electronic payment, consumers purchase electronic "coins" or "tokens" and use these specially marked and encrypted coins to make purchases.

Both systems have their advantages and disadvantages, just like credit cards and cash. Credit card encryption schemes are convenient and don't ask customers to change their usual purchasing methods. Transactions are charged to the credit card and appear on the customer's credit card statement just as any other purchase does. Electronic cash is a little less convenient, because customers have to buy electronic currency before they can use it. But electronic currency brings a certain amount of privacy to electronic purchases, particularly for pay-as-you-use services, such as online game playing.

URLs of Note

The Information Economy, prepared by Hal Varian at the University of California, Berkeley, covers the economics of the Internet and other issues: **http://www.sims.berkeley.edu/resources/infoecon/.**

Articles on network payment mechanisms and digital cash can be found at this site: **http://gauges.cs.tcd.ie/mepierce/project/html.**

CyberCash, a leading developer of secure payment services, can be found at this site: **http://www.cybercash.com/.**

VeriFone is working with browser software companies to deliver a secure payment network: **http://www.verifone.com/.**

How Electronic Cash and Credit Card Encryption Work

The most convenient way to pay for goods online is to use a secured payment network that encrypts your personal financial information so that it remains private as it passes through the Internet.

Download Helper App
(Not necessary if browser has built-in encryption)

Send Set-up Information

1 First, the customer must download an electronic payment helper app to use when shopping on the Web with "electronic cash." Some browser software already includes this app. The helper app includes an encryption key that encodes personal financial information so that it can only be decoded by the electronic payment service using a special second key.

Internet

Sample Browser: How the World Wide Web Works

Destination http://www.sample.com/samples/sample.html

HOW
Credit Card Encryption Works

123456789

Electronic Pay Helper Application

123456789 **Insert Encryption Key**

3 When a customer makes a purchase, the encrypted payment information is sent along with the purchase order to the merchant. Information is encrypted by applying a unique key to scramble the information. This scrambled information can only be descrambled by using a special second key.

6 The merchant receives verification in a matter of seconds and then can fulfill the order and send the goods to the customer.

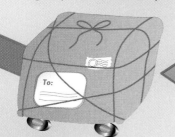

To:

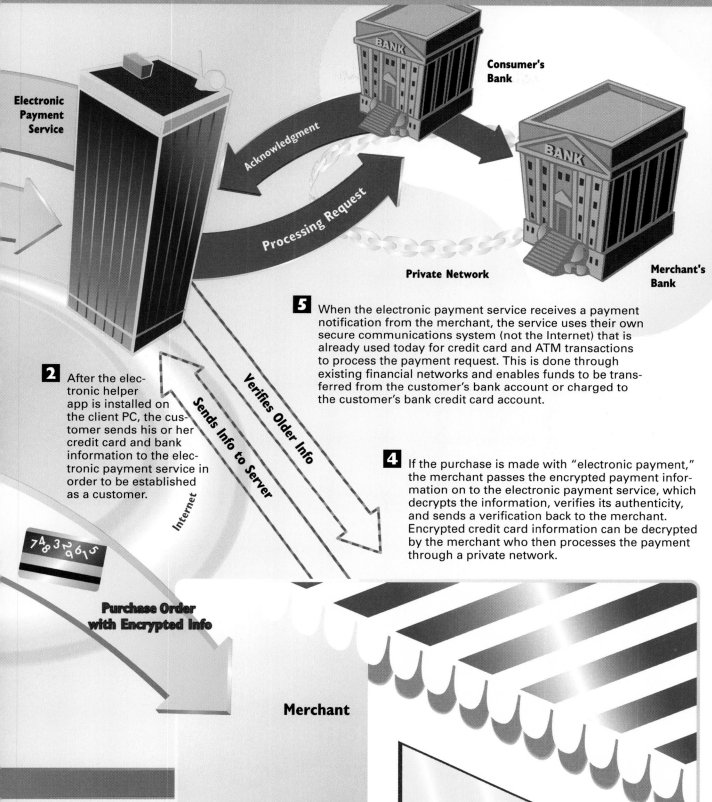

Electronic Payment Service

Acknowledgment

Processing Request

Consumer's Bank

Private Network

Merchant's Bank

5 When the electronic payment service receives a payment notification from the merchant, the service uses their own secure communications system (not the Internet) that is already used today for credit card and ATM transactions to process the payment request. This is done through existing financial networks and enables funds to be transferred from the customer's bank account or charged to the customer's bank credit card account.

2 After the electronic helper app is installed on the client PC, the customer sends his or her credit card and bank information to the electronic payment service in order to be established as a customer.

Verifies Older Info

Sends Info to Server

Internet

4 If the purchase is made with "electronic payment," the merchant passes the encrypted payment information on to the electronic payment service, which decrypts the information, verifies its authenticity, and sends a verification back to the merchant. Encrypted credit card information can be decrypted by the merchant who then processes the payment through a private network.

Purchase Order with Encrypted Info

Merchant

How Anonymous Payment Works

Anonymous payment schemes, such as Ecash developed by DigiCash, NetCash developed at the University of Southern California, and the PayMe Transfer Protocol, all enable customers to pay for items (information, services, or hard goods) using a private and secure method of transferring funds.

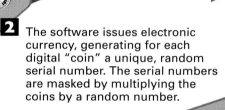

2 The software issues electronic currency, generating for each digital "coin" a unique, random serial number. The serial numbers are masked by multiplying the coins by a random number.

1 An electronic "wallet" helper app is used to purchase electronic currency from a "bank," then pay for items using this electronic money. The bank may be an actual banking institution or a payment processing center. In either case, the customer makes a withdrawal from the bank using the wallet software.

3 The coins are packaged into a message, digitally signed by the user's private identification key, encrypted with the bank's key, and sent to the bank. Only the bank can decrypt the message.

Payment Request

Paid $100

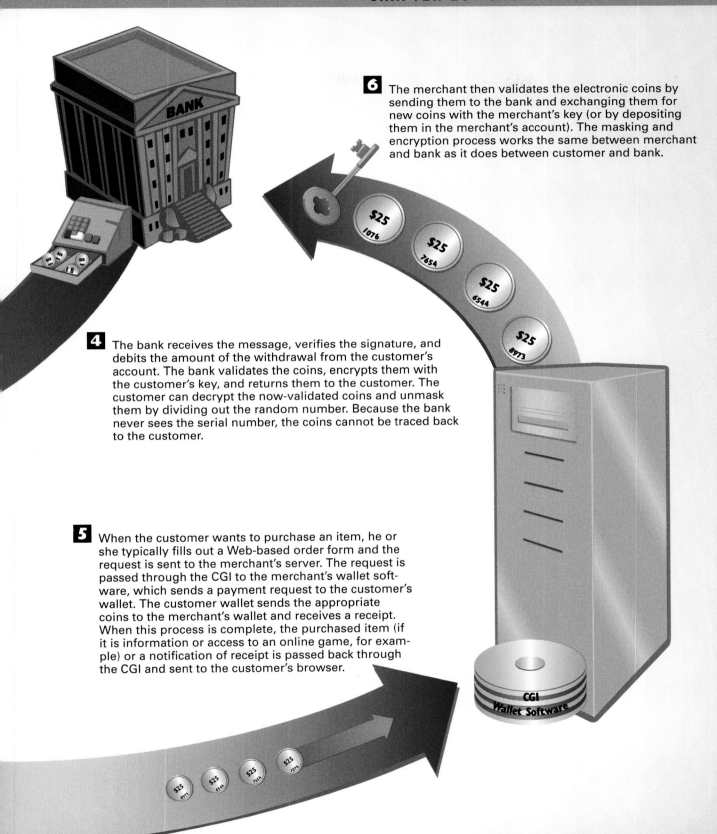

6 The merchant then validates the electronic coins by sending them to the bank and exchanging them for new coins with the merchant's key (or by depositing them in the merchant's account). The masking and encryption process works the same between merchant and bank as it does between customer and bank.

4 The bank receives the message, verifies the signature, and debits the amount of the withdrawal from the customer's account. The bank validates the coins, encrypts them with the customer's key, and returns them to the customer. The customer can decrypt the now-validated coins and unmask them by dividing out the random number. Because the bank never sees the serial number, the coins cannot be traced back to the customer.

5 When the customer wants to purchase an item, he or she typically fills out a Web-based order form and the request is sent to the merchant's server. The request is passed through the CGI to the merchant's wallet software, which sends a payment request to the customer's wallet. The customer wallet sends the appropriate coins to the merchant's wallet and receives a receipt. When this process is complete, the purchased item (if it is information or access to an online game, for example) or a notification of receipt is passed back through the CGI and sent to the customer's browser.

21

Security
on the Web

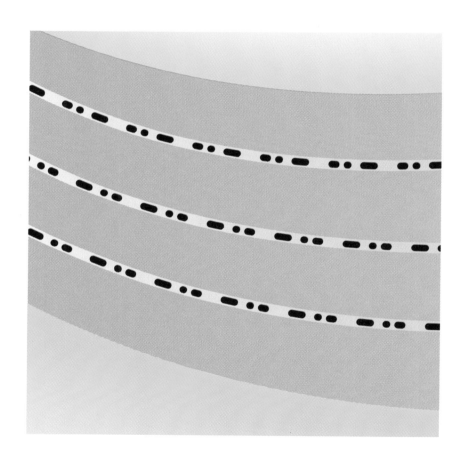

SECURITY

on the Web is becoming more important as businesses and organizations with private networks set up public Web servers. A public server can open up a can of worms for private networks because a computer thief could use the Web server as a gateway into the private network and the confidential records stored there.

Moreover, confidential documents stored on a company Web site could be at risk of being accessible to someone outside the organization. Also, private information sent from the client browser to the server could be intercepted through the opening created by a public Web server. This could be especially damaging to a company if credit information is revealed or other transactions are tampered with. Information is power. Any information coming out of the server's host computer about the server could be just the ticket for a cyber-thief to break down the door. Opportunistic hackers could cause a security breach by modifying the host computer using a CGI application. Intruders who know about the complex inner workings of a Web server, have the tools they need to manipulate the computer system for malevolent purposes.

A *firewall* is a security feature that blocks unauthorized communication between an independent network and the Internet. There is a greater security risk when a Web server is linked to a private network because server software can give dishonest users a window into the private computer system. Network administrators put the public Web server on the outside of the firewall to protect against this risk. When the firewall is between the public server and the private network the server is evocatively called "the sacrificial lamb." The Web server may be open to intrusion and hacking while the private network is safely behind locked doors.

Many vendors have developed enhancement schemes for HTTP that use *cryptography*. Cryptography—also called encryption—is a way to scramble electronic transactions mathematically. Such enhancements present various solutions for the problems of Web security. A company called EIT developed the *Secure Hypertext Transfer Protocol*, or S-HTTP. Created in early 1994, S-HTTP encrypts transactions at the application level. That means both browsers and servers write and recognize cryptography programs and passwords.

For example, if you are banking online or ordering with your credit card, the transactions between your client browser and the server must be encoded so no unauthorized users can read or tamper with them. Encryption technology uses a mathematical formula called an algorithm with a large randomized number called a key. The technology calculates the algorithm with two key numbers: one to encrypt the data and the other to decrypt it. These are referred to as "private" and "public" keys respectively. When the secure document reaches its destination, a public key is used to unscramble the document by recalculating the algorithm.

The relative security of encryption keys is proportional to the length of the keys. For example, a four-digit key is child's play to a skilled hacker compared to a 120-digit key. The length of these keys is measured in bits, so 4-bit is 16 digits and 8-bit is 256 digits. Any encryption greater than 40-bit is considered a "munition" by the U.S. Defense and Justice Departments and is illegal to export. Most security measures currently on the Internet use keys of 40 bits or less because of this restriction. A 40-bit key may sound like maximum security, but in cryptography circles keys of less than 120 bits are not considered to be totally secure.

The simplest type of security feature is still a shared secret, usually a password. When you create a password, or if one is created for you, the Web server's host computer keeps it on a list with all users' passwords. Password lists are usually not encrypted, so don't be lulled into feeling totally safe. Yet if you make a truly unique password this system will keep some intruders at bay. When creating your own password use numbers and letters (both upper- and lowercase) and try to avoid information that can be easily acquired or deduced, such as your birth date or middle name.

Passwords are often used on registered Web sites. A registered site asks you to create a user name and password for yourself on your first visit. On subsequent visits you must log in when prompted by typing your user name and password. You can change your password at any time after you have logged in. It is a good idea to change passwords weekly or monthly, if only to create a moving target for gate-crashers trying to break into the host system using your identity. Registered sites keep track of usage, which is convenient for commercial sites that want to track the number of hours a user spends at their site. Other registered Web site servers will "remember" you from visit to visit, keeping track of your preferences and surfing habits. Information unique to you is collected on a database and stored until your next login. Remember that your name and other information collected on registered sites can be legally sold by the owners of that site to a third party. Do not register information on these Web sites that you want to keep totally private.

URLS of Note

The archive of the Web security mailing list, in which members discuss how they address security concerns, can be found at this site: **http://asearch.mccmedia.com/www.security.html/**.

A comprehensive Web site addressing an array of security issues: **http://www.genome.wi.mit.edu/ WWW/faqs/www.security.faqs.html/**.

To learn more about Secure HTTP, visit this Web site: **http://www.eit.com/projects/s-http/ index.html/**.

How Firewalls Work

Web servers can present some security concerns to companies or groups that wish to keep private documents out of public hands. A firewall system can prohibit unauthorized access to sensitive files.

2 Other private networks have a gateway through the firewall so users on the local network can access the Web and other information on the Internet. This is like a small crack in the security dam that only allows limited types of connections to outside networks. However, system administrators can use passwords and other security measures to log into the private network from an outside location.

1 A business or organization may have a self-contained network that is inaccessible from the Web and the Internet. This is called a private network. Users within the private network can share information with each other but not with computers outside the network.

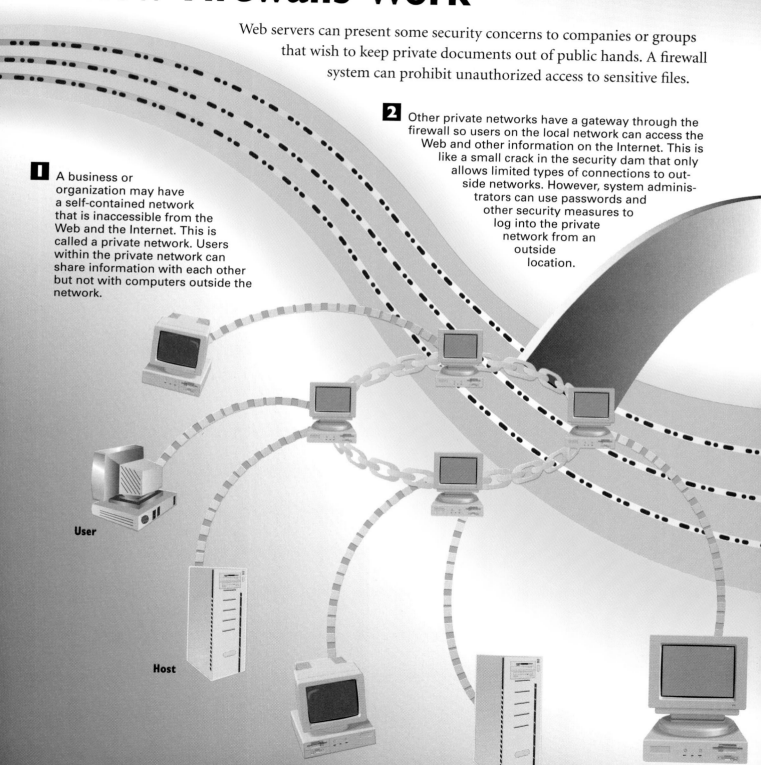

User

Host

3 The firewall is a computer system that limits access to a network to authorized personnel. It also may let private network users through to access the Internet or surf the Web.

Firewall Machine

Host Machine for Web Server

The World Wide Web

4 A business or organization with a Web server may elect to place the host computer outside the firewall or set up a freestanding machine with no connection to the corporate network. This allows the outside world to access public Web pages without strict security clearance.

Public Networks

Firewall

Web Note

When the Web server is placed outside the firewall, it opens the possibility of hackers tampering with the host machine. The thinking behind this approach is that intruders may sabotage the Web server and its host machine, but at least the server doesn't open a window into the organization's private network and confidential documents. Sensitive documents living on the private network will be safer behind the firewall. Public documents that reside outside the firewall on the Web server are less secure.

Private Networks

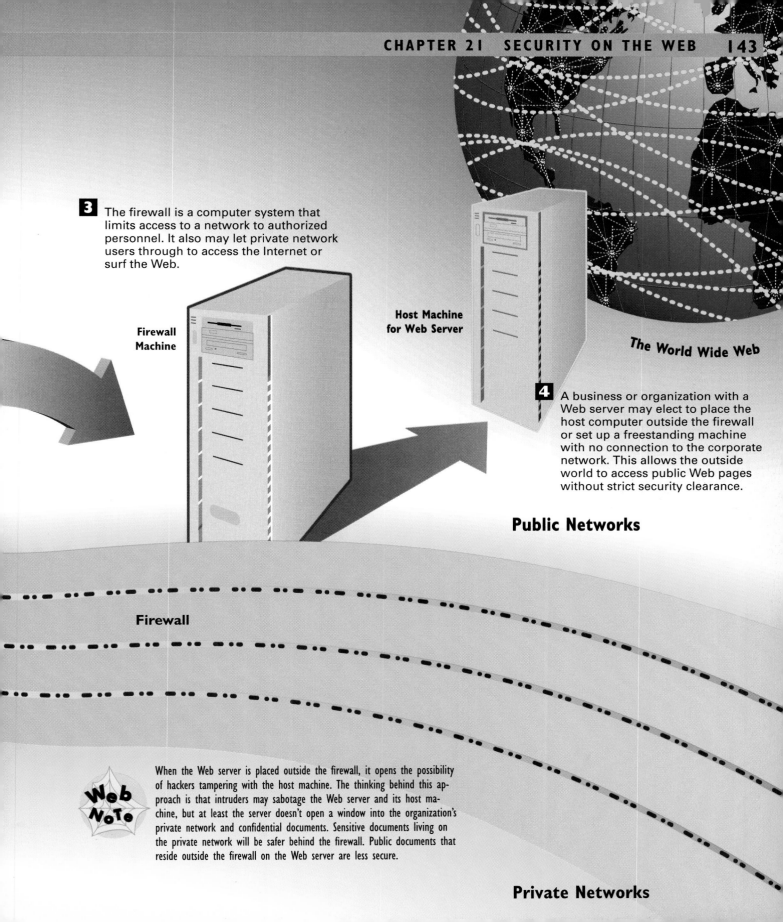

CHAPTER
22

Keeping Kids Safe on the Web

THE biggest controversy to hit the Web is described variously as the "free speech" issue or the "pornography" problem. No matter what you call it or where you stand, the fact is that sites throughout the Web contain material that may be considered offensive, obscene, and unsuitable for minors.

Some people believe the First Amendment protects Americans' right to place whatever material they choose on the Web. Others believe that material deemed obscene should be prohibited from publication on the Web. The debate has been going on for quite a while, but it got an extra stir when Congress passed and the president signed the Telecommunications Act of 1996. The Act contains a provision that makes it a federal offense to use an "interactive computer service" to publish material that is "obscene or indecent" knowing that the material may be accessible to minors. The somewhat vague language of the Act, as well as its intent, has people on all sides of the issue arguing in court about the validity of this section of the law. In the meantime, a number of organizations have developed rating systems and technology protocols to help parents decide what they do and do not want their children to see on the Web. Regardless of the outcome of the public debate, it's clear that these techniques are applicable *now* and they place the responsibility for and the decisions about children's access to the Web squarely in the hands of parents.

Leading this effort is SafeSurf, a parents' organization that, along with an Internet industry-wide group, developed a rating system and encoding scheme called the PICS (Platform for Internet Content Selection) protocol. PICS combines a standard template for rating the content of a Web site with a coding scheme that embeds the rating into an HTML page. In this way, PICS-enabled browsers can read the rating code, and depending on the screening settings established by the browser owner, determine if the page will be displayed. In short, the SafeSurf Internet Rating Standard and the PICS protocol combine to give parents a way to designate what their children can and cannot see when they access the Web.

The Internet Rating Standard is implemented through MIME types called applications/pics-service and applications/pics-labels. Remember that a MIME (Multipurpose Internet Mail Extension) is a technique for sending information about data across the Internet as part of the message header. By creating a MIME to identify the content label of a Web page, the browser can filter out unwanted content. The *service* MIME type is the URL of an individual, group, or company that provides content labels for information on the Internet and Web. The *content label* provides information about a page's contents, and has three parts: the URL of the rating service, a set of PICS-defined attributes that provide information about the rating (such as the date the rating was assigned), and a set of ratings-system defined attributes that actually rate the content in specified *categories,* such as violence, vocabulary, or sexual content. These categories are defined by the rating service.

One such rating service is the Recreational Software Advisory Council (RSAC), which created a system that includes three categories: violence, nudity/sex, and language. Each category is rated on a scale from 0 to 4. Each value has an assigned meaning, but generally the 0 indicates no violence, for example, and 4 represents extensive violence.

The SafeSurf standard for identifying and rating content has been adopted by a wide range of companies, including Microsoft, which has promised to incorporate a PICS-compliant rating system in its Internet Explorer browser included in Windows 95. Other PICS-compliant browsers aimed specifically at the family market include Net Nanny Ltd.'s Net Nanny, Microsystems' Cyber Patrol, TeacherSoft's InterGO, and Solid Oak's CYBERsitter.

In addition to using a PICS-compliant browser, there are other things for parents to consider when their children go online. Most commercial online services include parental controls that can be used to prevent children from using certain aspects of the service, such as chat rooms, Internet newsgroups, and the service's Web browser.

Parents can also set some "online rules" for kids, with guidelines and time limits for online access, and remind children never to give their real full name, home address, or telephone number or to agree to meet in person someone they met online. Parents can't always be at their children's side when the kids are online, but they should occasionally join in a surf session and ask kids about the things they have discovered online.

SafeSurf even encourages parents to have an "online agreement" with kids, asking kids to tell a parent when they find information online that makes the child feel uncomfortable, telling parents about people they meet online, and promising not to respond to e-mail from strangers or to provide personal information to people online.

The Web offers a great deal of fun and educational content designed especially for children. Parents can support and encourage their children in discovering this vast opportunity for learning by using some common sense—and the technology available in PICS-compliant browsers—to keep kids safe.

URLs of Note

A number of companies offer tips for online safety, as well as information about their Web site screening software. These are just a few of the Web sites available. This list doesn't imply an endorsement of products, but rather offers avenues for further exploration.

SafeSurf describes its Internet Rating Standard and provides tips for keeping kids safe on the Web: **http://www.safesurf.com/**

Platform for Internet Content Selection is the working body creating a standard for content rating: **http://www.w3.org/PICS**

Microsytems' Cyber Patrol provides a free demo version of their screening software: **http://www.microsys.com/CYBER/**

Trove Investment Corp.'s Net Nanny provides information about screening software along with a free demo version of its software: **http://www.netnanny.com/netnanny/**

SurfWatch Software's SurfWatch promotes free speech on the Web and provides product information and demonstration: **http://www.surfwatch.com/**

Net Shephard Inc.'s Net Shepard provides information about their browser add-in product: **http://www.shepherd.net/**

There are hundreds of Web sites specifically designed to be fun and educational for kids. Here are a few we found, and you'll also want to check out your favorite Web directory for more:

Maddy Mayhen's Kids Stuff is a bright, entertaining front door to lots of kid-friendly Web sites created by a mother and her six-year-old daughter: **http://wchat.on.ca/merlene/kid.htm**

The New Castle-Henry County Public Library in New Castle, Indiana, maintains this annotated list of kid-appropriate sites called Kid's Hits: **http://www.nchcpl.lib.in.us/Library/LibraryInfo/KidzHitz.html**

Aha! is a fun-filled site created by the Emmy award-winning producer of Captain Kangaroo, Sesame Street, and other children's programming: **http://www.aha-kids.com/**

The National Football League created this site to introduce kids to the sport and its star players called NFL kids: **http://nflhome.com/kids/kids.html**

How PICS Works

PICS—the Platform for Internet Content Selection—includes a rating system and an HTML encoding scheme that lets PICS-compliant browsers filter out Web pages that parents deem inappropriate for their children.

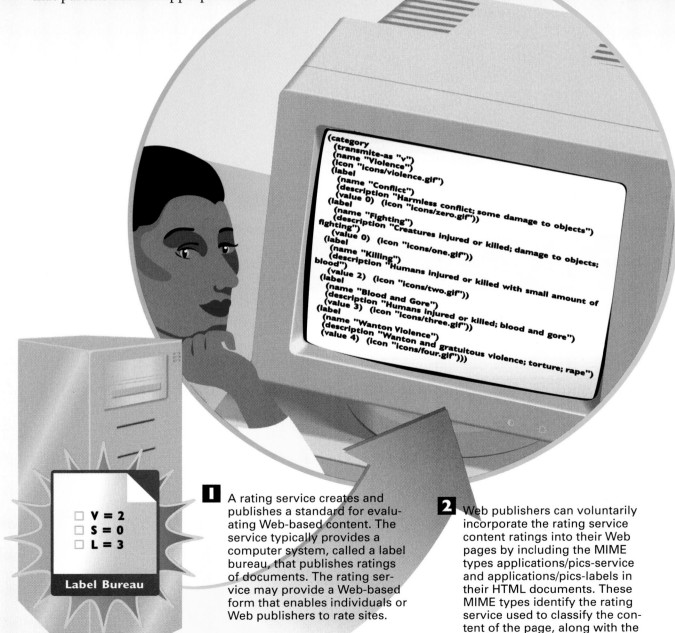

```
(category
  (transmit-as "v")
  (name "Violence")
  (icon "icons/violence.gif")
  (label
    (name "Conflict")
    (description "Harmless conflict; some damage to objects")
    (value 0)  (icon "icons/zero.gif"))
  (label
    (name "Fighting")
    (description "Creatures injured or killed; damage to objects; fighting")
    (value 0)  (icon "icons/one.gif"))
  (label
    (name "Killing")
    (description "Humans injured or killed with small amount of blood")
    (value 2)  (icon "icons/two.gif"))
  (label
    (name "Blood and Gore")
    (description "Humans injured or killed; blood and gore")
    (value 3)  (icon "icons/three.gif"))
  (label
    (name "Wanton Violence")
    (description "Wanton and gratuitous violence; torture; rape")
    (value 4)  (icon "icons/four.gif")))
```

☐ **V = 2**
☐ **S = 0**
☐ **L = 3**

Label Bureau

Rating Service

1 A rating service creates and publishes a standard for evaluating Web-based content. The service typically provides a computer system, called a label bureau, that publishes ratings of documents. The rating service may provide a Web-based form that enables individuals or Web publishers to rate sites.

2 Web publishers can voluntarily incorporate the rating service content ratings into their Web pages by including the MIME types applications/pics-service and applications/pics-labels in their HTML documents. These MIME types identify the rating service used to classify the content of the page, along with the ratings themselves.

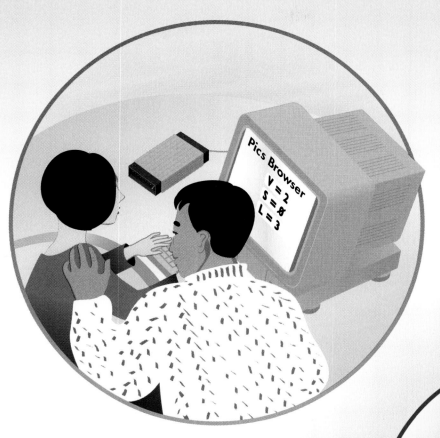

3 Parents can configure PICS-compliant browsers to filter Web pages according to their content ratings.

4 When a Web page is received, the client browser scans the rating label values to be sure that they match the criteria set by the filter. Pages with appropriate ratings are displayed, while those that do not meet the criteria are not.

CHAPTER

23

Planning Your Own Web Page

THE personal computer revolution—much like the invention of the printing press—gives tools of expression and distribution to a growing number of people. Information and knowledge are at your fingertips—and you can contribute! The Web can be your personal soapbox, where you are free to offer insights about a hobby, advertise your business, or simply express your opinions. For relatively little money, you can post vast amounts of information on the Web. But the same capabilities that let people express themselves has, unfortunately, allowed a lot of useless material to be posted on Web servers around the world. Make your Web site distinctive. Try to contribute pages that are neat and to the point. A sharp focus will make for a more lively and potent message.

Make a plan for your site. This step is often called *storyboarding*, a term borrowed from film-making. Planning a site will help you arrange the pages logically so users will not be confused or get "lost" when browsing through your site. The first page people will see is called a welcome page. You should give your welcome page the file name *index.html* because Web browsers open *index.html* by default. Following this convention will also make your URL easier to remember and share with others.

HTML editors are often helpful when creating Web pages. Some software, such as Adobe's PageMill, produces simple HTML tags for your documents. This will save you time and effort of learning HTML. An HTML generator like PageMill may be a cost-effective solution if you are posting many simple Web pages. However, you can create fine Web pages with any text editor, even a simple one like Windows NotePad.

Once you have created an HTML page you will probably want to punch it up with pictures, graphics, and icons. Many simple icons and images are freely available from the Internet. (Please observe all trademark and copyright laws.) When choosing colorful icons, bullets and bars, re-member that brevity is a virtue. A good GIF—the standard Internet image format—is worth a thousand words, unless it is too large and takes minutes to download. Keep the file size small when you are creating or modifying an image by reducing the range of colors and its dimensions. Many Web page designers use a technique on their GIFs called *interlacing*. An interlaced GIF will load either as a very low-resolution image that slowly comes into focus, or like venetian blinds that fill in small vertical sections. This way the image is partially visible even before it is completely downloaded.

Another common design technique is to make your GIFs transparent. A transparent GIF often looks good because it integrates with the background of a page. Imagine a square image with a globe in the center and black around the edges. When you link to the globe image it is dis-played as a black square with a globe in the middle. You may want to show the globe on your

Web page without the black edges. To do this, make a transparent GIF and select black as the transparent color. Whatever is underneath the transparent color will show through, so you see just a globe and no black square.

It is helpful to put the graphics for your Web page into a directory or folder called "graphics" or "images" or the like. This makes it easier to find and change your images after you post them to a Web server.

You can preview your new Web pages at this stage. Using any Web browser simply open your local HTML document with the "open file" command. The browser will parse and display your page just as it would a page retrieved from the Web. You can easily make modifications to the graphics and the HTML, then reload the page to verify your changes are correct.

The first version of your Web page is done, and you are ready to show it to the world. Now what? First, you must have access to an HTTP server or, with the right hardware, software, and connection, you can set up a server yourself. Maintaining your own server is a large commitment of money and time, but it provides much more control. If you are planning to post many pages of information—about your business, for example—or if you need to make extensive use of interactive forms, then it may make sense to set up your own server.

Server setup requires that you or your system administrator configure it—adjust its settings—to fit your needs. Server software such as Quarterdeck's WebStar for Macintosh or WebServer for Windows can be installed quite easily. The programs have a graphical interface that make setup reasonably easy. It is best to have at least one computer and phone line dedicated to the task of serving Web pages. Your local phone company can arrange for a special high bandwidth phone line that is always connected to the Internet or service provider. This is called a *dedicated* or leased line. A dedicated line is essential because the server computer must stay on and the phone line open if you want your pages to be accessible around the world at any time. In most cases, your server will only serve files. Other users on the Web will find your server through another computer on the network called a domain name server (DNS). Domain name servers allow users to find your site with domain names like www.zdpress.com instead of numerical IP addresses.

A simpler solution is to rent space on a server from an Internet Service Provider, or ISP. Many ISPs include some disk space for posting pages as part of their service. In this case, the ISP will usually create a directory or folder for you on their HTTP server. This folder will be given your user name (something like mfish) and is often preceded by a tilde (~, the character to the left of the exclamation point on your keyboard) to indicate a shortcut to this folder. You will put your new HTML document and graphics into that folder just as you arranged them on your own hard drive. If you named the first-level document index.html then your URL could look like this: http://www.myISP.com/~my_username/.

To put your work on an ISP's server you must transfer the files over the Internet. One of the best ways of doing this is with an FTP program like Anarchie (Mac) or FTP32 (Windows). If you are using a UNIX machine, use the built-in FTP. Once you put a file on the server it will be available for all to see. If you have a PPP or SLIP connection to the Internet, your FTP program should do the rest. First, open your personal folder located on the server. You will need the user name and password given to you by the ISP. Then simply put your HTML document into that folder, followed by your images or the folder that contains all the images. The files will transfer from your computer's hard disk to the server's hard disk. Once they arrive, anyone surfing the Web should be able to see your work. You should test your pages now that they are "live" to check for any "bugs," or errors in the HTML coding. Remember that UNIX and the Web are case-sensitive and do not recognize spaces, so incorrect capitalization or spacing within file names will cause errors.

How Web Sites Work

Making your own Web page is becoming easier every day. You may want to teach yourself HTML basics, but software is now available that allows you to make pages without any HTML experience. Once you create your pages you can post them with FTP software onto a small portion of a Web server. You can either rent the server space from a local ISP or set up your own Web server.

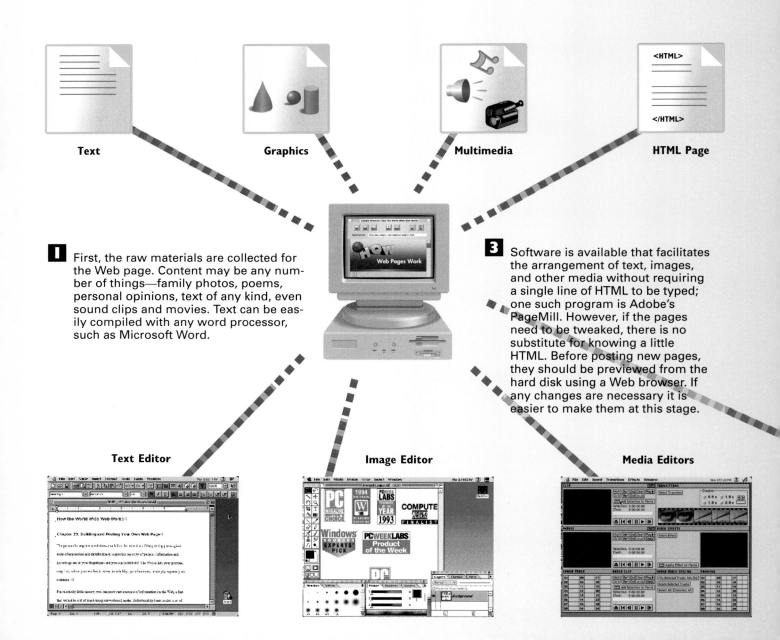

Text

Graphics

Multimedia

HTML Page

1 First, the raw materials are collected for the Web page. Content may be any number of things—family photos, poems, personal opinions, text of any kind, even sound clips and movies. Text can be easily compiled with any word processor, such as Microsoft Word.

3 Software is available that facilitates the arrangement of text, images, and other media without requiring a single line of HTML to be typed; one such program is Adobe's PageMill. However, if the pages need to be tweaked, there is no substitute for knowing a little HTML. Before posting new pages, they should be previewed from the hard disk using a Web browser. If any changes are necessary it is easier to make them at this stage.

Text Editor

Image Editor

Media Editors

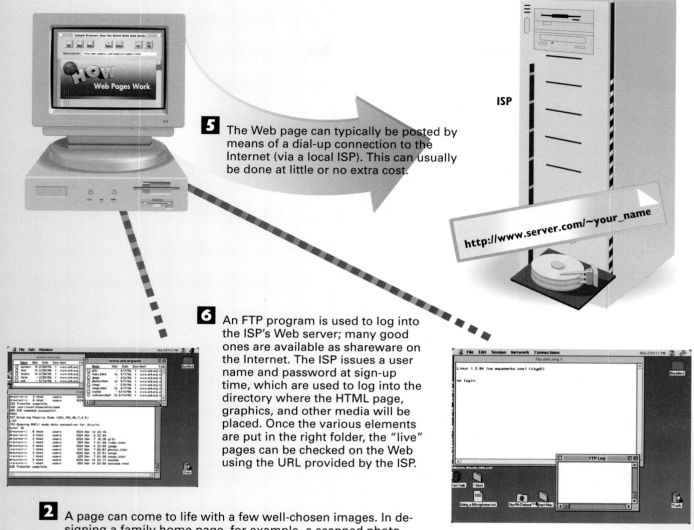

5 The Web page can typically be posted by means of a dial-up connection to the Internet (via a local ISP). This can usually be done at little or no extra cost.

ISP

http://www.server.com/~your_name

6 An FTP program is used to log into the ISP's Web server; many good ones are available as shareware on the Internet. The ISP issues a user name and password at sign-up time, which are used to log into the directory where the HTML page, graphics, and other media will be placed. Once the various elements are put in the right folder, the "live" pages can be checked on the Web using the URL provided by the ISP.

2 A page can come to life with a few well-chosen images. In designing a family home page, for example, a scanned photo might work well on the Web page. Icons or colored bullets spruce up a text list, and navigational icons such as arrows or pointers let a user move logically around the site. A whole range of shareware image editors is available on the Internet. The most full-featured commercial image editor is Photoshop by Adobe. Photoshop is a professional-grade program that allows you to modify, create, or resize virtually any digital image.

HTML Editor

4 If you want to add other media to your pages, such as digitized sound, music, or video, you will need access to the digital files or you can digitize it yourself with additional computer hardware. When you are dealing with media with large file sizes—like a 4MB movie—it will take users a very long time to download the file. During editing, try to trim all the fat out of video and audio clips. Also try to scale back the length and resolution of audio and video to decrease file size.

CHAPTER

24

How Intranets Mirror the Internet

INTRANETS are among the hottest topics discussed in corporate board-
rooms these days. The thinking goes something like this: Let's
use the same efficient, relatively low-cost technology to share information *inside* the company
that we're using to share information with people *outside* the company. An intranet, essentially,
is a mini-Internet contained within a corporate enterprise. An intranet may ultimately link to the
broader Internet, but it doesn't necessarily have to.

Intranets make a lot of sense in today's larger, rapidly evolving businesses, especially those
with branches around a city, around the country, or around the globe. These businesses are constantly creating and disseminating information to their employees. Corporate announcements,
policy and procedure documents, human resources information, company forms, pricing lists—
all of this information and more needs to get into the hands of employees quickly. Too often,
though, policies change even as new handbooks are being printed. Employees may find themselves working from differing, and sometimes outdated, data sheets. Thousands of forms are
printed, only to be destroyed when new versions are issued.

In order to manage this morass of essential information, companies seek out a central information repository, housing a single copy of the most up-to-date documents. Corporate databases
and information-management products such as Lotus Notes were supposed to provide this information storehouse—and they do. But many companies have found these systems to be expensive
to install, difficult to learn, and costly to maintain. Enter an intranet.

An intranet relies on the same basic technology that companies use to implement their Web
sites. By creating an Internet-like infrastructure on top of the organization's existing local area
networks, and by providing employees with low cost, easy-to-use browsing software, businesses
are finding the "in-house Web" to be a cost-effective, efficient solution to their corporate communications problems.

The basic intranet configuration (assuming an organization already has a local area network
in place) consists of Web server software and server hardware with a network card that supports a
TCP/IP connection to the client PCs on the network, and Web browser software for the networked
client PCs. Many companies are opting for a Windows NT server because their organizations
have already standardized on the Windows platform and it is usually familiar to the information
services personnel, but UNIX-based Web servers are also an option. Additionally, companies will
need the software-appropriate tools to create the Web content, provide searching capabilities,
and integrate existing databases with the new intranet.

Certainly it will take some time and effort to place company documents on an intranet, but
adding HTML markups to existing documents is generally not a difficult proposition. Moreover,

intranet-based documents can create other efficiencies, in addition to keeping documents updated. For example, rather than distributing paper-based forms, a company can use their intranet as a data collection system. So, for instance, human resources forms can be accessed and filled out by employees on the intranet and the information will be deposited directly into the HR databases, keeping corporate files updated and eliminating the delays and errors of paper-based systems.

The intranet can also ensure that all employees, whether they are at the home office or a remote location, are receiving the same up-to-date information. Imagine how useful it will be for sales representatives to access the corporate intranet to get the latest pricing schedules, rather than relying on weeks-old price sheets.

The intranet doesn't have to be an island, though. Intranets can be linked to the broader Internet to give Web access to all or to selected employees. Of course, companies that link their internal network to the Internet will need to take measures to secure the corporate systems. That's where the firewalls and other security technologies discussed in Chapter 21 come in.

Because they can be created with a relatively low investment in new technology, and because they can start out slowly and grow as needed, intranets are the most rapidly growing use of Internet technology in corporations today—and ironically they may not even be part of the Internet at all.

URLs of Note

The Intranet Journal is an independent publication exploring the tools that serve the internal commmunications needs of businesses. It can be found at **http://www.brill.com/intranet/.**

WebMaster magazine maintains a Web site devoted to the issue of Intranetwork: **http://www.cio. com/WebMaster/wm_irc.html/.**

Internet Advisor magazine covers a variety of issues, including Intranets, and posts back issues on its Web site: **http://www.advisor.com/ia.html/.**

How Intranets Work

An intranet relies on Internet communications technology to create a mini-Internet within a corporate enterprise.

An intranet is built on top of existing local area network technology, adding server hardware and Web server software to host an internal Web site (or multiple Web sites).

Intranets use the same TCP/IP protocols to send requests and data between the client and host computers that the Internet does.

Web Server IP Address 123.45.67.8

The intranet host server has a unique IP address that enables the client PCs running Web browser software to locate the server on the network.

Local Area Network

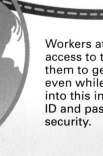

Workers at remote locations can have dial-in access to their company's intranet, enabling them to get up-to-the-minute information—even while at a client site. Users who dial into this intranet must have a network login ID and password to ensure corporate data security.

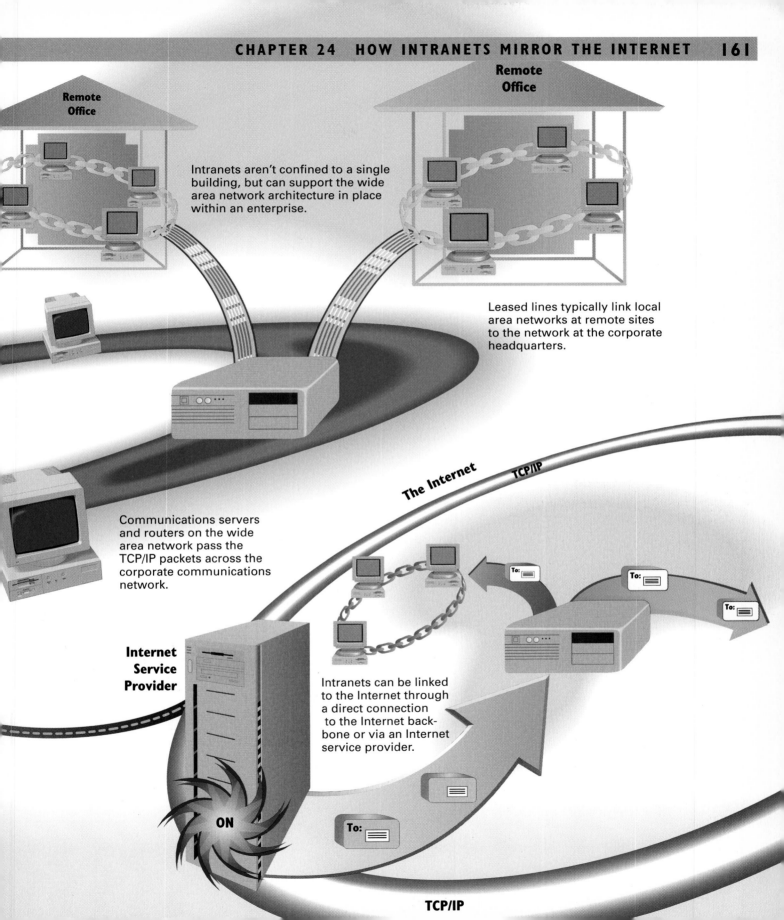

Remote Office

Remote Office

Intranets aren't confined to a single building, but can support the wide area network architecture in place within an enterprise.

Leased lines typically link local area networks at remote sites to the network at the corporate headquarters.

The Internet   TCP/IP

Communications servers and routers on the wide area network pass the TCP/IP packets across the corporate communications network.

Internet Service Provider

To:

To:

To:

Intranets can be linked to the Internet through a direct connection to the Internet backbone or via an Internet service provider.

ON

To:

To:

TCP/IP

INDEX

Note: Italicized page numbers refer to illustrations.

X

Y